THE BEDFORD SERIES IN HISTORY AND CULTURE

Street Life in Renaissance Rome

A Brief History with Documents

Related Titles in
THE BEDFORD SERIES IN HISTORY AND CULTURE
Advisory Editors: Lynn Hunt, *University of California, Los Angeles*
David W. Blight, *Yale University*
Bonnie G. Smith, *Rutgers University*
Natalie Zemon Davis, *University of Toronto*

THE BEDFORD SERIES IN HISTORY AND CULTURE

Street Life in Renaissance Rome

A Brief History with Documents

Rudolph M. Bell

Rutgers University

BEDFORD / ST. MARTIN'S   Boston ◆ New York

For Bedford/St. Martin's

Publisher for History: Mary V. Dougherty
Director of Development for History: Jane Knetzger
Senior Editor: Heidi L. Hood
Developmental Editor: Debra Michals
Production Supervisor: Victoria Sharoyan
Senior Marketing Manager: Paul Stillitano
Editorial Assistant: Laura Kintz
Project Management: Books By Design, Inc.
Cartography: Mapping Specialists, Ltd.
Permissions Manager: Kalina K. Ingham
Text Design: Claire Seng-Niemoeller
Cover Design: Marine Miller
Cover Art: A Street Scene with a Capriccio of Roman Buildings (oil on canvas),
   Lingelbach, Johannes (1622–1674)/Worcester Art Museum, Massachusetts, USA/
   The Bridgeman Art Library.
Composition: Achorn International, Inc.
Printing and Binding: RR Donnelley and Sons

President, Bedford/St. Martin's: Denise B. Wydra
Presidents, Macmillan Higher Education: Joan E. Feinberg and Tom Scotty
Director of Marketing: Karen R. Soeltz
Production Director: Susan W. Brown
Associate Production Director: Elise S. Kaiser
Manager, Publishing Services: Andrea Cava

Library of Congress Control Number: 2012942563

Manufactured in the United States of America.

7   6   5   4   3   2
f   e   d   c   b   a

For information, write: Bedford/St. Martin's, 75 Arlington Street, Boston, MA 02116
   (617-399-4000)

ISBN 978-0-312-62297-8

Acknowledgments

Acknowledgments and copyrights are continued at the back of the book on page 157, which constitutes an extension of the copyright page. It is a violation of the law to reproduce these selections by any means whatsoever without the written permission of the copyright holder.

Foreword

The Bedford Series in History and Culture is designed so that readers can study the past as historians do.

The historian's first task is finding the evidence. Documents, letters, memoirs, interviews, pictures, movies, novels, or poems can provide facts and clues. Then the historian questions and compares the sources. There is more to do than in a courtroom, for hearsay evidence is welcome, and the historian is usually looking for answers beyond act and motive. Different views of an event may be as important as a single verdict. How a story is told may yield as much information as what it says.

Along the way the historian seeks help from other historians and perhaps from specialists in other disciplines. Finally, it is time to write, to decide on an interpretation and how to arrange the evidence for readers.

Each book in this series contains an important historical document or group of documents, each document a witness from the past and open to interpretation in different ways. The documents are combined with some element of historical narrative—an introduction or a biographical essay, for example—that provides students with an analysis of the primary source material and important background information about the world in which it was produced.

Each book in the series focuses on a specific topic within a specific historical period. Each provides a basis for lively thought and discussion about several aspects of the topic and the historian's role. Each is short enough (and inexpensive enough) to be a reasonable one-week assignment in a college course. Whether as classroom or personal reading, each book in the series provides firsthand experience of the challenge—and fun—of discovering, recreating, and interpreting the past.

Lynn Hunt
David W. Blight
Bonnie G. Smith
Natalie Zemon Davis

Preface

The Renaissance is alive and well. After several decades of disparagement and even dismissal, very recent scholarship seeks to return the era to its former prominence in the history of Western civilization. *Street Life in Renaissance Rome* aims to bring this newly invigorated view into the classroom. Instead of highlighting only the glories of artistic and literary achievement, it reflects the new scholarship by including the lives of ordinary people. A firm and lasting assessment of the Renaissance requires us to dig deeply into the human sweat, exploitation, and chicanery that coexisted with the pomp and grandeur. Doing so is the purpose of this volume.

The earlier view of the Renaissance, for reasons explored more fully in the introduction, overlooked the experiences and struggles of servants and unskilled laborers, of wives and daughters, and of marginalized groups such as Jews and prostitutes. It concentrated on Florence and on relatively homogeneous urban centers such as Urbino and Arezzo, where there was little ambiguity about Renaissance achievements, rather than on Rome. The streets of the Eternal City—as ancient Romans confidently called the home they thought would last forever—provide an ideal locale for a wider perspective. They are where high culture met low, where great artistic and intellectual achievements stood alongside food hawkers, fishmongers, and the homeless. The examination of life in public spaces in this collection of documents conveys a more complete history of the Renaissance as it was experienced by most Romans.

A second feature of this volume is the extension of coverage from the Renaissance into the Reformation in order to support instructors who need to treat both periods in a short amount of time and with reading assignments of reasonable length. Rome had been the capital of the lost world of antiquity to which the Renaissance gave rebirth, but equally it was home to the papacy and the center of the Christian world sundered by the Reformation. In the overlapping eras, tens and even hundreds of thousands of visitors and pilgrims came each year to Rome, Europe's largest gathering place. They commented freely on what they saw and heard: the vagaries and varieties of daily life in the streets and piazzas. The documents in this volume include selections from the works of distinguished theologians, scholars, and artists while showcasing as well the largely forgotten thoughts of people whose everyday lives enrich our traditional understanding of the Renaissance, the ordinary folk who toiled in shadows cast by the era's architectural triumphs and who could neither read its literary masterpieces nor gain access to view its paintings and sculptures. From this composite record a vivid portrait emerges of what it was like to be a Renaissance man or woman walking Rome's streets, gathering at its parades, celebrating its carnivals, and avoiding the dangers of its criminals and its squalid, disease-ridden quarters. Along with the volume's primary focus on the Renaissance, the inclusion of documents featuring the writing of Erasmus, Valdés, and Luther should also stimulate discussion of the Reformation.

Street Life in Renaissance Rome is divided into two parts: an introduction that provides context for understanding Rome's rich street life and a collection of primary source documents that give voice to daily life. The introduction sets forth a broad periodization for the Renaissance from its beginnings in the early fourteenth century, when the city was temporarily neither the capital of Christendom nor a splendid place to visit, through the glory years of pageantry devastatingly brought to a halt by the sack in 1527, and on for another century during which Protestants and Catholics fought over their versions of Christianity, punctuated by the formal dedication of St. Peter's Basilica in 1626. Following a brief explanation of how historians have defined the Renaissance and why definition matters, the introduction returns to the people of Rome, describing their places in the pyramid structure of its economy and in its highly gendered social order. Prelates, prostitutes, and Jews vie for the students' attention in ways not found in the usual textbook treatment of the Renaissance. The introduction then shifts to key political themes: the decline of civic authority in the early years, the sundering of Christendom with the challenges initiated by Martin Luther in 1517, the failure of the papacy to defend its secular power a decade later on the battlefield of Rome's streets, and finally the late-sixteenth-century renewal of the Roman Renaissance as an essential component of Catholicism's response to the Protestant Reformation.

Part Two of this book contains documents selected to highlight and deepen the themes and particulars set forth in the introduction. The documents are organized in sections that address the beginnings of the Renaissance, the lives of Renaissance Romans, visitors to Rome, the sack of Rome, and voices of the Reformation. The selections continue to portray Renaissance Rome from the vantage point of the street and through the eyes of the people who walked there: women down on their luck, pilgrims and curiosity seekers, penniless talented artists with huge egos itching for a fight, Jews trying to stay safe by keeping low profiles, and legions of churchmen whose ungodly behavior shocked even the most hardened visitors. The individual documents offer a wide variety of genres: poetry, dialogue, an advice manual, short fiction, a song, letters, biography and autobiography, trial records, a papal bull, a household inventory, historical accounts, a travel narrative, and diaries.

The variety of primary sources encourages students to appreciate the kinds of materials historians use as they attempt to understand a fascinating era such as the Renaissance. The nature of these sources is especially important in the difficult task of recovering the history of ordinary people during this tumultuous time, especially for historians who seek to document the lives of the nameless men and women who served the needs of the great artists, illustrious scholars, and powerful prelates. The pages that follow include women's voices that were so long ignored in the litany of Renaissance giants as well as the voices of formally ostracized groups such as Jews and of informally ignored people, including the homeless, streetwalkers forced by circumstances to sell access to their bodies, and marginalized petty thieves and muggers who made Rome's streets notoriously dangerous. The discourses of Protestant and Catholic reformers are also present, allowing for discussion about critical themes in sixteenth-century religious history, with the focus on Rome and the papacy again allowing for illuminating commentary.

The documents in this volume do not include reproductions of Renaissance art and architecture, although the introduction does provide a tantalizing portrait of Pope Julius II attributed to Raphael. A single slim volume cannot do everything, and the choice here is to emphasize written works directly related to recovering the lives of ordinary Romans, leaving to Internet access the visual cultural artifacts that are abundantly available there in full color.

Following Part Two, readers will find additional pedagogical material: a chronology with key markers of the long Renaissance presented in this volume, a set of initial questions for further discussion of issues raised by the documents, and a bibliography of English-language sources that are readily available and highly readable for students seeking to explore more fully this fascinating era.

Illustrative material providing pedagogical support begins with a map of Rome as a frontispiece to the introduction that portrays three interrelated ways for students to orient themselves spatially: (1) Rome's census districts, which reflect the city's social and economic divisions; (2) major monuments and piazzas that are as eagerly sought by tourists today as they were during the Renaissance; and (3) the zones of high population density crowded along the Tiber River, equally the gathering point for rich and poor. The introduction also includes two pieces of great art, both deeply layered with hidden meanings and contradictions about life in Renaissance Rome: the Capitoline She-Wolf and Raphael's portrait of Pope Julius II. Also featured in the introduction are two contemporary photographs, one of the Forum of Augustus and the other of a statue of Pasquino, each of which illustrates the complexities of a city that lived on and for its ancient ruins, infusing them with highly contested and ever-changing meaning over the past two millennia.

ACKNOWLEDGMENTS

My thanks go first to my colleague Bonnie G. Smith, who encouraged me to turn the bundles of assorted documents and excerpts I kept in a file drawer labeled "Renaissance Rome" into a reader from which students and teachers well beyond my own classroom might benefit. She introduced me to Mary Dougherty, Bedford/St. Martin's publisher for history, who convinced me to write this book. Freelance editor Debra Michals provided editorial supervision for the book with superb skill, great patience, and keen interest. Several reviewers provided useful feedback. I appreciate especially the suggestions by Tovah Bender, Agnes Scott College; Pietro Frassica, Princeton University; Nichola Harris, Ulster County Community College; Martha Howell, Columbia University; Jennifer McNabb, Western Illinois University; Duane Osheim, University of Virginia; and Amanda Pipkin, University of North Carolina, Charlotte. Laura Kintz at Bedford/St. Martin's greatly eased the challenges of obtaining permissions to include various documents and illustrations, and Nancy Benjamin of Books By Design did splendid work in the final stages of production.

Ana Jimenez Moreno, then an outstanding Rutgers undergraduate honors student and currently a literary scholar at Notre Dame, contributed greatly to the project from the outset. Beyond the essential work of locating, scanning, proofreading, correcting, formatting, word counting, and initiating permissions for the various selections, she engaged in highly informative exchanges about which potential selections were lively, readable, boring, too long, too short, crucial, informative, essential, or redundant—and why. In the fall of 2009 I also tested the choice of selections with a focus group formed by the forty students registered in my History of Italy's Peoples class. Their oral responses, as well as written results from an essay question I put on their take-home final exam, fine-tuned the selections. For translations of several documents I turned to Martina Saltamacchia, a native Italian speaker with a wonderful sense for poetic and early Italian usages, who currently teaches history at the University of Nebraska at Omaha. I thank her as well for her many suggestions. I am grateful also to my colleague David Marsh for tracking down several especially obstinate Roman literary usages. I appreciate the excellent advice Donald Kelley gave me about the Erasmus and Luther document selections. Precious assistance on the illustrations came from art history experts Joseph Consoli, Tod Marder, and Erik Thuno and for technical work on the map from Isaiah Beard, James Hartstein, and Ronald Jantz at the Rutgers Library Scholarly Communications Center. For the actual photographs I am pleased to mention the artistic skill and friendship of Cristina Mazzoni (Figure 1) and Martina Saltamacchia (Figures 2 and 4).

A NOTE ABOUT THE TEXT

Square brackets in the texts indicate editorial additions to the original document either to give context for parts of a selection or to clarify a translation. Dates given in the headnote are for the original document, not the edition or translation provided. Martina Saltamacchia provided original translations of the following documents:

Document 3, Catherine of Siena, *Letter to Pope Gregory XI*, ca. September 13, 1376

Document 4, Giovanni Mattiotti, *Francesca Romana*, ca. 1440

Document 6, *Song of the Penitential Lay-Sisters Gone to Rome*, Fifteenth or Sixteenth Century

Document 7, *Pasquinades*, Sixteenth Century

Document 9, Alessandro Trajano Petronio, *On Roman Lifestyle and the Preservation of Good Health*, 1592

Document 23, Caspar Schoppe, *Letter to Conrad Rittershausen on Giordano Bruno*, February 8, 1600

Rudolph M. Bell

Contents

Map and Illustrations

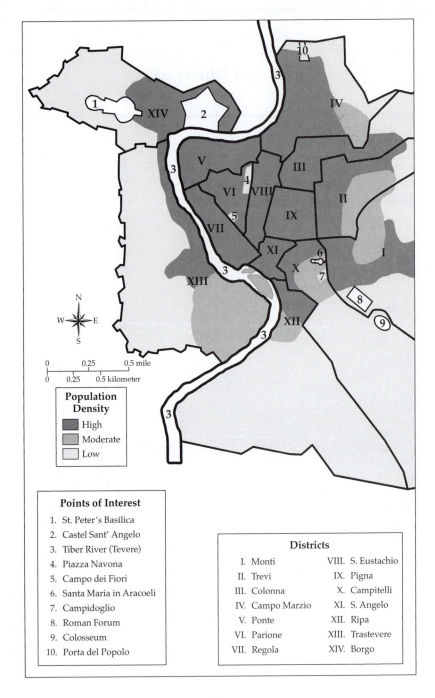

Population Density
- ■ High
- ▨ Moderate
- ☐ Low

0   0.25   0.5 mile
0   0.25   0.5 kilometer

Points of Interest
1. St. Peter's Basilica
2. Castel Sant' Angelo
3. Tiber River (Tevere)
4. Piazza Navona
5. Campo dei Fiori
6. Santa Maria in Aracoeli
7. Campidoglio
8. Roman Forum
9. Colosseum
10. Porta del Popolo

Districts

I. Monti	VIII. S. Eustachio
II. Trevi	IX. Pigna
III. Colonna	X. Campitelli
IV. Campo Marzio	XI. S. Angelo
V. Ponte	XII. Ripa
VI. Parione	XIII. Trastevere
VII. Regola	XIV. Borgo

PART ONE

Introduction:
Rome—An Untold Story

A conventional history of Renaissance Rome might begin in 1453, with Pope Nicholas V's (r. 1447–1455) coronation of Frederick III as Holy Roman emperor. It would continue with Pope Sixtus IV (r. 1471–1484), who initiated an artistic renaissance in Rome that included restructuring the civic piazza of Campidoglio, building a new bridge over the Tiber River, and constructing the Sistine Chapel. It would mention his sponsorship of the Roman Academy, devoted to the revival of classical, pre-Christian scholarship, which formally reconvened in 1478, thus reversing the antihumanist suspicions of his predecessor, Pope Paul II (r. 1464–1471). Such a history would feature Michelangelo's completion in 1541 of *The Last Judgment* fresco on the altar wall of the Sistine Chapel, and the controversy it ignited among Catholic Reformation prelates offended by its nudity. It might end with the formal dedication of the monumental St. Peter's Basilica in 1626, a time when the Catholic Church seemed to have regained much of its former vigor. A conventional history would also note the Protestant Reformation, with its irreparable breakdown of Western Christendom, and would include a few words on the 1527 sack of Rome, but primacy would likely be given to the monumental artistic geniuses whose works define this era, Donato

---

Opposite: **Map.** *Renaissance Rome*
The map locates elements of the three foundational legacies of Western Christendom that uniquely came together in Renaissance Rome: legendary founding, Antiquity, and Christianity itself. District outlines and population density shading provide further information.

Bramante, Michelangelo Buonarotti, and Raffaello Santi (Sanzio; known as Raphael) among them.

While the 1626 dedication of St. Peter's Basilica works as an end date for Rome's Renaissance, this book starts in 1309, when even the papacy had abandoned Rome. The earlier start best suits the different account of Renaissance Rome offered here. Although artistic achievements are mentioned in passing, this history instead emphasizes the daily lives of ordinary citizens, the plight of social outcasts, and the dangers of urban life. Both histories are true, and they depend upon each other; the first has often been told, and the second needs to be heard. This second history not only gives a more balanced portrait of the Renaissance as experienced by the vast majority of Romans at the time, but it also invites a new understanding of the Renaissance in northern Italy and throughout Europe as more than a florescence of high culture.

Rome, the Eternal City, was preeminent among Western Christendom's capitals, rivaled by no other European city for its sacred past and vibrant present. Pilgrims hoping for miraculous cures crossed paths with diplomats on critical missions of war and peace. High prelates drawn to the pleasures and profits of worldly power and scholars searching for rare manuscripts mingled at the Vatican's earthly gates. An endless assortment of adventurers, students, artists, poets, tricksters, ne'er-do-wells, and curiosity-seekers were among the throngs of visitors. Abandoned women seeking a fresh start in life crowded into the tightly packed quarters along the Tiber, especially where the river wound around the papal fortress of Castel Sant' Angelo.

All three of the legacies historians usually define as critical in shaping Western civilization flourished within the boundaries formed by Rome's ancient aqueducts. In chronological order, the first of these legacies is local (indigenous) tradition, in Rome's case its mythical founding in 753 BCE by the brothers Romulus and Remus. Antiquity constitutes the second legacy, especially the glorious centuries of the Roman Republic and Roman Empire that stretched over the better part of a thousand years and centered on the city's seven fabled hills. The third legacy, Christianity, had been initiated with St. Peter's Roman bishopric and the apostolic tradition of continuity from Christ to the living pope, and it guaranteed Rome's claim to supremacy in the Western world. All three legacies were intensely focused on the physical place that was Rome and were constantly being reimagined on its streets and in its artistic treasures, making the city an ideal venue for understanding the varied and contested meanings of the Renaissance, a key period in Western civilization.[1] Rome's great artistic achievements came while ordinary folks led tumultuous lives on the streets and behind the doors of humble dwellings. By exploring their experiences, this book widens the portrait both of Rome itself and of the Renaissance writ large.

Although elements of the three foundational legacies of Western civilization might be found anywhere in Europe, nowhere else did they join in such dynamic contrast and in such visible ways as they did in Rome. As to traditions based in the indigenous culture, England had its Stonehenge mysteries, Ireland its fanciful leprechauns, and northern Europe its gold-hoarding Nibelungs and the Valkyrie Brynhildr, but none of these traditions appeared in ubiquitous representations on city streets and certainly not side-by-side with edifices from antiquity and monuments of Christianity. Rome was unique in that its traditions were visible everywhere.

Travelers to Renaissance Rome, who are heavily featured in Part Two (Documents 12, 13, 14, 15, 21, and 22), invariably climbed the Capitoline Hill, central among the city's famed seven hills and the locus of its secular politics, to a crowning piazza known in guidebooks of the time and today as the Campidoglio. There they gazed upon one of the world's most famous sculptures, the fiercely protective she-wolf guarding the infant twins Romulus and Remus as they grasped for milk. The babies were said to have been born to a vestal virgin named Rhea Silvia, a descendant of Aeneas, a hero of the Trojan war. Legend says that the boys' father was Mars, god of war, and that they were a product of his rape of Rhea Silvia. Her brother, fearing revenge for earlier familial assassinations, snatched the infants and abandoned them on the banks of the Tiber, where they were rescued by the thirsty wolf. The twins grew up, murdered their evil uncle, and established themselves at what would become Rome, whereupon the younger boy, Romulus, yet a teenager, killed his older brother in order to rule the new city on his own.

The she-wolf sculpture and the violent story behind it radiate with ambiguities, innuendos, and contradictions that may serve as a provocative way to introduce Renaissance Rome: maternal nurture; familial assassinations; vigilant predators; bloodthirsty men; nature tamed, but also exposed and inscrutable. Both Rhea Silvia's vow of virginity and its violation by the god of war tell us of male domination and exploitation, a Renaissance theme about which the documents in this book have much to say (especially Document 11). Finally, there is the sculpture itself, long asserted to have been carved around 500 BCE by an unknown Etruscan master, which would make it a stunning artistic accomplishment for the people who inhabited central Italy well before the first arrival of Greeks on the peninsula. Recent scientific carbon dating, however, suggests that the Capitoline masterpiece may have been created no earlier than the thirteenth century, and the playful twins are certainly

Figure 1. *Capitoline She-Wolf*
Palazzo dei Conservatori, Musei Capitolini, Rome. The date of this statue's
creation is disputed (traditionally Etruscan fifth century BCE, but uncon-
firmed carbon testing puts it as late as the thirteenth century, with the twins
added even later). Like Renaissance Rome itself, the statue seems old and also
new as it reflects ambiguity, mystery, power, and elegance.

a later addition to the original bronze sculpture. Nothing in Renaissance
Rome was as it appeared from a single angle or upon first glance, a truth
nicely embodied in the sculpture of the she-wolf and its relocation in
1471 by Pope Sixtus IV from St. John the Lateran to the Capitoline Hill.[2]
  A Renaissance visitor who turned from the she-wolf to gaze toward
the southeast could not possibly miss the gigantic Colosseum, a massive expression of Roman antiquity, the second foundation of Western
civilization, standing less than a mile away. More immediately below
the Campidoglio stood defiant columns amid a shamble of stones in the
narrow valley between the Capitoline and Palatine hills. In that place the
ancient Roman Forum, a complex of civic buildings, markets, and sites
of worship, had once stood. Masterpieces of antiquity remained elsewhere in Europe, of course, sometimes in ensembles better preserved
than those of Rome—for example, the Acropolis in Athens and the

Valley of the Temples in Agrigento—but nowhere else did the interplay of the indigenous, the ancient, and the Christian foundations of Western civilization so powerfully and simultaneously appear.

As with the she-wolf, even the seemingly obvious contained contractions and ambiguities. The Renaissance tourist who looked closely at the Colosseum saw gouged-out holes that once held bronze hinges that subsequently were melted down for the fashioning of Christian icons. Such vandalism made the blocks of stone that tumbled to the ground easier to cart away for new building projects. Not until 1749, when Pope Benedict XIV (r. 1740–1758) decided that the martyrdom of early Christians sacrificed to hungry lions and other beasts within the amphitheater by pagan Romans made it a holy space, did the destructive quarrying stop. No such link to Christian tradition existed for the temples, sanctuaries, shops, and government buildings of the Roman Forum, and their fate during the Renaissance is what the observer sees today—a place overrun by stray cats, covered with uncultivated plant life, and strewn with human detritus.

Turning counterclockwise, the Renaissance pilgrim would have encountered a monumental expression of the third foundation of Western civilization—Christianity. She or he would have been atop steps leading to Santa Maria in Aracoeli, where in 1354 Cola di Rienzo, the radical demagogue who sought to restore Rome to its ancient grandeur, met his death, after which his body was desecrated by a mob instigated by the powerful Colonna family (Document 2). As with so much else in Rome, below the surface were complex layers of past reality, each shaping the meaning of the present. The Church of Santa Maria in Aracoeli had been a favorite of Cola's, and he had enhanced its entry with the magnificent 124-step staircase that ultimately became the place of his assassination. In its earlier renditions, the church had been the central mint for Roman coinage, a religious temple, and a place where seers assembled to predict the future by studying birdcalls and flight paths. In a tragic irony, when the resurgent Roman Republic sought by Cola di Rienzo briefly became a reality under Napoléon I in 1797, the French conquerors turned his prized church into a stable.[3]

The physical realities of Rome perplexed, amazed, disgusted, and inspired the throngs of visitors, none more so than Dante Alighieri, author of the *Divine Comedy,* hailed as the literary work that defined the Italian language. The poem captures the complexity and ambiguity of Rome's self-image in its opening part, the *Inferno.* As Dante and his guide Virgil enter the first *bolgia* (pocket) of the eighth circle of hell, where seducers and panderers receive their just punishments, the Florentine poet invokes a direct comparison of the horrifying scene with

what he may have witnessed on the streets of Rome in the Jubilee year of 1300:

> All of these sinners were naked; on our side
> of the middle they walked toward us; on the other,
> in our direction, but with swifter stride.
> Just so the Romans, because of the great throng
> in the year of the Jubilee, divide the bridge
> in order that the crowds may pass along,
> so that all face the Castle as they go
> on one side toward St. Peter's, while on the other,
> all move along facing toward Mount Giordano.[4]

Dante's invocation of a Roman procession as he explores the depths of hell is no accident. More shocking, or perhaps more scandalous to the city's visitors than any other aspect of Rome's street life, were the huge numbers of pimps, courtesans, and *puttane* (whores) who strolled about the city, especially along the Tiber. One mid-sixteenth-century tourist, the Englishman William Thomas (Document 12), noted forty thousand as the number of Rome's female sellers of sex, surely an exaggeration in a city of less than a hundred thousand people, but other observers penned equally harsh commentaries (Documents 1, 17, 18, 19, and 22).[5] The point seems to be less the accuracy of these estimates and more the impression that the city's streets left on visitors.

Despite the fascination with and descriptions of women as sexual objects, the image of women as saviors of mankind always coexisted. Later in the *Divine Comedy*, Dante hailed Rome's soil as nurturing the roots of the tree of good and evil. Even Christ was a Roman, the poet wrote in Canto XXXII of the *Purgatorio* as he readied himself for his journey from Purgatory into Paradise. At this point, in a literary variation of the antiquity-Christianity interplay found everywhere in Rome's architecture, Dante had to leave Virgil behind and continue his journey

---

Opposite: **Figure 2.** *The Forum of Augustus*
This photograph displays the historical layers in which Rome was built, which are still visible simultaneously, as they were during the Renaissance. Ruins of the Forum of Augustus are in the foreground, with the House of the Knights of Rhodes, constructed in the twelfth century and heavily redesigned in the fifteenth century, on the left behind the rubble. To the right is the wall that originally separated the Forum from the ancient Roman lower-class red-light district of Subura, known as the Monti district in Renaissance times. Beyond and to the right is the thirteenth-century Tower of the Militia.

with Beatrice, a holy female, as his guide. Woman might be blamed for Man's downfall, but she was also his savior:

> Here briefly in this forest shall you dwell;
> and evermore, with me, be of that Rome
> in which Christ is a Roman.[6]

Never more than during the Renaissance did Rome's streets teem with awe-inspiring contrasts. A tradition of public spectacle played out in open spaces crowned with bizarrely incongruous Egyptian obelisks, monumental pagan sculptures, and dazzling fountains, attracting throngs of visitors. They saw the crumbled Roman ruins, courtesans flashing sumptuous silks and jewels, and the courtesans' unwanted daughters, who had been rescued by the Jesuit school at S. Caterina dei Funari, parading to the Chiesa del Gesù dressed as heroic martyr saints. They saw cardinals galloping on mighty steeds, muggers lurking in alleyways, vendors peddling elixirs guaranteed to restore youthful vigor, and proper matrons seeking indulgences by making arduous visits to seven or even forty-nine designated churches. In 1527 they saw the city sacked by rampaging foreign troops. Public life in the streets of Renaissance Rome reflected the virtues and vices of Western Europe. The people—Jews and Christians, Italians and foreigners, clerical and secular, wealthy and poor, powerful and forsaken—gazed upon each other and upon an unending series of religious processions, festivals, carnivals, fisticuffs, murders, pillaging, partying, vending, and hustling.

Romans applauded their popes for ongoing spectacles of street theater. An informative if gruesome example may be found in the punishment that Pope Leo X (r. 1513–1521) imposed in 1517 against several of Cardinal Alfonso Petrucci's minions. The jealous cardinal had been charged with plotting to bribe one of the pope's physicians to poison the ointment used to relieve the pontiff's painful anal fistula. In recognition of Petrucci's high status, the record tells us, he was strangled privately with a cardinal-red cord by a swarthy Muslim, since no Christian could shed the blood of another, especially one so noble.[7] To the delight of a crowd of curious onlookers, two of his accused coconspirators were paraded through the city's streets on their way to a summary execution, while paid torturers ripped at their flesh with hot tongs.

This introduction and the documents in Part Two present Renaissance Rome's history through the eyes of its residents and visitors, men and women, high and low, peaceful and warlike. They witnessed the beautiful and the ugly, the sacred and the profane, the lofty and the desolate, making clear the many dimensions of the Renaissance itself.

DEFINING THE RENAISSANCE

First, however, it is important to examine the second key term in this book's title, *Renaissance*, literally "rebirth." The artist Giorgio Vasari, best known as the author of *Lives of the Artists* (1550), first used the term to describe the work of Tuscan artists and architects, starting with Cimabue (ca. 1240–ca. 1302) and focusing especially on Giotto (ca. 1266–1337). Vasari saw in their accomplishments a rebirth of classical forms of visual expression. Over the following three centuries, this rebirth matured in clearly defined phases beginning with the development of perspective and culminating in the ability of Michelangelo (1475–1564) to depict the human body in ways that surpassed even the masters of antiquity. The word *Renaissance* has remained relatively uncontested among art historians, who use it today to designate work outside the chronologically overlapping Gothic tradition and before the Baroque, roughly from 1300 to 1650, with allowance for the designation of Mannerism in late Renaissance painting. The interests of this book are wider.

Beyond the specific concerns of the visual arts, the term became more powerful with Swiss historian Jakob Burckhardt's publication of *The History of the Renaissance in Italy* (1860). Burckhardt defined the Renaissance as a crowning period in the history of Western civilization, expanding beyond art and architecture to include the literary and philosophical developments that later came to be known as Renaissance humanism. He emphasized a certain "spirit of the time," a worldview of Renaissance men (stating incorrectly and without evidence that women enjoyed full equality in this era). Unlike their medieval predecessors, he asserted, Renaissance explorers, inventors, conquerors, and architects had confidence in their ability to shape their world and to determine the future. Christopher Columbus sailing westward toward unknown shores, Leonardo da Vinci attempting to fly, Hernán Cortés seeking gold in Mexico, and Filippo Brunelleschi building a gravity-defying dome in Florence—such individual endeavors familiar to every European and American student ultimately came to epitomize the Renaissance.

In the immediate aftermath of the Second World War, this narrative of European triumphalism filled a contemporary void, as new ways of learning from the past seemed essential in combatting the legacies of Nazism and communism. An intellectual link between the Renaissance and the Protestant Reformation came to make sense. The underlying assumption about both eras was that human beings, thinking and acting independent of scriptural authority and in defiance of a no-longer-universal Catholic Church mired in the Dark Ages, controlled their destiny and shaped the future. Increasingly in the late 1960s, however, historians began to question the prevailing laudatory view of the Renaissance. First of all, who paid for all the artists and poets? A century earlier, Karl Marx had looked closely at the era and found in it the origins of capitalism. But modern critics concluded that the Renaissance grew to maturity in the decades of misery before and after the 1347 outbreak of plague known as the Black Death, flourished during a period of fierce competition for resources as Europe sought global expansion and the defeat of Islam in the fifteenth century, and reached new heights in a sixteenth century marked by famine, pestilence, destructive warfare, and the permanent fracture of Western Christendom into rival Protestant and Catholic creeds.

Scholars now question the proper place in our historical understanding for the ordinary people whose Renaissance lives consisted of hard toil in the fields to supply food for the idle rich, of backbreaking labor to build the city palaces, and of empty promises of God's salvation proclaimed by clerics in brocaded robes. Surely the humble people also had a worldview, one more likely captured in the residues of local oral traditions and in the trial records kept by defensive male witch-hunters and inquisitors intent on casting all dissent as heresy than in the humanist's treatise or the playwright's farce. While recent scholarship has rescued the spirituality and artistic accomplishments of a significant number of women from the historical dustbin (Documents 3, 4, and 11), the now-prevailing view remains that the Renaissance saw a hardening of gender discrimination, with declining roles for women in politics, the economy, and the public sphere.[8] Even in the home and in the quest for personal salvation, Protestant and Catholic Reformation theology and practice oppressed women. Protestants curtailed devotion to Mary, the mother of Jesus, and forbade the intrusion of saints into popular religion, avenues of pious expression that had been important for medieval women (Documents 3 and 4), and Reformation Catholic male clerics grew deeply suspicious of female spirituality expressed outside the convent. While unending doctrinal disputes even to the present day between Protestants and Catholics guaranteed that the Reformation would continue to be defined as a universally accepted epoch of importance in Western civilization, by the 1980s the term *Renaissance* came perilously close to vanishing, or at best to being dismissed as a derogatory label for a passing moment, among elite men.

This book accepts the word *Renaissance* as a vital way to understand the period from the early fourteenth through the early seventeenth centuries, but it builds upon the critics of the past fifty years who have argued that a place must be found not only for the accomplishments of the few but also for the daily lives of the many. Knowing not only about the creativity but also about the labor that went into a Renaissance canvas or façade deepens our overall appreciation of artistic greatness as well as our understanding of the past from a multitude of perspectives. Some of the documents in Part II flowed from the pens of men hailed as Renaissance geniuses, but even in these selections (especially Documents 18 and 19) the emphasis is on the small joys and endless challenges of daily life among the people of Rome.[9]

A PYRAMID OF RENAISSANCE ROME'S PEOPLES

Who were the Romans, the men and women rendered poetically by Dante as the brothers and sisters of Christ? The image of a pyramid may be helpful. At the top of the apex stood the pope, formally known as the Bishop of Rome. The pope was elected by the College of Cardinals, often with much chicanery and little concern for holiness, to serve until his death. The city also hosted an elite class of nobles, most with familial names continued from antiquity. Their wealth and prestige were based largely in the surrounding countryside, and they were generally content to leave civic display and power to the pope. The base, consisting of many layers—all beholden for their livelihood in one way or another to the high clerics and nobles at the apex—included the vast majority of Roman citizens and resident foreigners. Famous artists belonged here, at least economically (Documents 10 and 11), as did thousands of day laborers whose names appear only fleetingly in the occasional census. The excluded, whether formally discriminated against as in the case of Jews (Document 8) or rendered invisible in most historical narratives as were women engaged in the lower rungs of the sex trade (Documents 6 and 17), tell us much about the vicissitudes of life in these troubled times.

With the exception only of a small minority of long-established noble families who chose to reside in town, Renaissance Rome was a place of foreigners. Rome's highly open and varied population gave the Eternal City a key aspect of its international lure. Setting himself apart from the negative consensus expressed by medieval Frankish visitors who had crossed the Alps,[10] the widely traveled sixteenth-century Frenchman Michel de Montaigne (Document 15) observed that Rome was "of all towns in the world, the one most filled with the corporate idea."

He explained that here "difference of nationality counts least; for, by its very nature, it is a patchwork of strangers, each one being as much at home as in his own country." Neighborhoods did tend to self-segregate by place of origin, or in the case of Jews were forcibly ghettoized, but when strolling along the streets and gathering in the piazzas, everyone was a Roman because no one was a Roman (Document 13, Sonnet 78).

The Apex

As were most of Rome's people, the man at the very top of the pyramid, the pope, was only infrequently a Roman by birth. More often, a new pope brought in and surrounded himself with a huge entourage of trusted fellow townsmen whose loyalties were seldom intertwined with those of the city's ordinary denizens. Beyond being the Bishop of Rome, he was the leader of a church whose confines went beyond the Eternal City. Among the thirty-five popes who served between 1378—the year after French Pope Gregory XI (r. 1370–1378) returned to Rome from Avignon, France, at the urging of future saint Catherine of Siena (Document 3)—and the formal dedication in 1626 of the new St. Peter's Basilica by Pope Urban VIII (r. 1623–1644), only three popes were born in Rome proper, with eight others hailing from various towns contained within the Papal States of central Italy. The remaining twenty-four were from foreign city-states or kingdoms: Florence four, Genoa four, Naples four, Milan three, Venice three, Siena two, Valencia two, France one, and the Holy Roman Empire one. Within this list of thirty-five, the first chronologically among the Renaissance popes native to Rome itself or the Papal States was Martin V (r. 1417–1431), born as Oddone Colonna of the ancient Roman noble Colonna family. He deemed Rome so unsafe and inhospitable that he chose to linger elsewhere for three years before taking up residence, leaving it to his soldiering brother Giordano to quell the factional warfare that roiled the city. Even then, Oddone Colonna stayed away from St. Peter's, spending most of his time at his familial palace across the Tiber while refurbishing the adjacent Church of the Twelve Apostles, or else sojourning in one of the countryside towns held by his family, upon whose members he lavished a multitude of ecclesiastical offices.

Even more notorious than Pope Martin V for the excesses of his nepotism was Roderic Llançol i Borja (Rodrigo Borgia), who reigned from 1492 to 1503 as Pope Alexander VI. He attained infamy during his lifetime for placing the interests of his illegitimate children above all other concerns, including those of the church and of the Roman people.

Cesare and Lucrezia (or Lucretia) Borgia and their father, Rodrigo, were immediately and forever after cast by onlookers as wicked practitioners of unbridled lust, incest, political intrigue, and murder by poisoning, and a full portrait of Renaissance Rome necessarily includes the stories surrounding them, which are replete with contradiction and irony (Document 5). Rodrigo adored Lucrezia, trusting her above all others and taking her advice even on matters of high state politics. Their relationship is in stunning contrast to the usual picture of Renaissance fathers who cared nothing for their daughters. As an intellectual, Lucrezia held her own in Italy's most refined courts and earned the admiration of literati such as Ercole Strozzi and Pietro Bembo, to whom she addressed what Lord Byron centuries later described as "the prettiest love letters in the world."[11] Her brother Cesare, the model for Niccolò Machiavelli's (1469–1527) ruthless ruler in his classic essay *The Prince* (1513), the most widely read of all Renaissance writings even to this day, may have murdered his brother in a living reenactment of the Remus and Romulus legend, but he was also a patron and friend to Leonardo da Vinci, employing the artist's services as an architect and engineer crucial in his military exploits. According to Machiavelli, Cesare Borgia might have succeeded in holding his kingdom in central Italy, and perhaps even in unifying the peninsula, had not ill fortune intervened in the person of Pope Julius II (r. 1503–1513), an implacable foe of the dead Rodrigo who by deception won Cesare's support for his election to the papacy. Famously depicted on a canvas attributed to the painter Raphael (Raffaello Santi or Sanzio da Urbino) as a pensive old man, Pope Julius II displays prominently and with firm hands the rings that symbolize his earthly power and sits on a throne adorned with the acorn symbol of his family crest. The grand trappings of papal power—the keys and the tiaras originally painted in gold on the background wall to the right—are visible, even though covered over by the artist with matching green. The visual trick, arguably intentional, masks only partially the warmongering side of Julius II that contemporary writer and theologian Desiderius Erasmus satirized with such savagery in his attack on the pope's corruption of Christ's message (Document 21). Even the pope's beard is temporary, grown as a penance for his defeat a year earlier in a battle to retain Bologna and shaved off shortly after Raphael completed this portrait. The eternal verdict on Pope Julius II is ambiguous, but in the history of Renaissance Rome the spiritual leader who sponsored three of its greatest artists—Bramante, Raphael, and Michelangelo—holds a permanent place of distinction.[12]

Figure 3. *Portrait of Pope Julius II,* 1511, by Raphael (Raffaello Santi or Sanzio da Urbino, 1483–1520)

As with the statue of the she-wolf (Figure 1), this painting simultaneously conceals and reveals by means of the symbols of power painted over yet visible on the background wall as well as by Pope Julius II's firm hand, more appropriate for a warrior than a spiritual leader.

The Base

Foreigners also figured largely in the multilayered base of Rome's population pyramid, men and women not so well documented on canvass and in historical annals who nonetheless contributed to what contemporary French essayist Montaigne termed Renaissance Rome's "corporate idea" and others would call its cosmopolitan style, verve, and danger. The best glimpse of the social composition of Rome's non-elite people is contained in a census undertaken in late 1526 or early 1527, shortly before leaderless and unpaid troops sent earlier by Holy Roman Emperor Charles V against French forces attempting to occupy parts of northern Italy marched south and sacked the city, dreaming of riches for the taking (Documents 16–20). Perhaps the officials in Rome had been anticipating a long siege rather than a violent frontal invasion. Whether the census had the benign purpose of estimating how much grain to store in case of a siege, or the equally plausible aim of counting households for some emergency tax, is unknown. Not everyone was counted accurately, the suspicion of a tax being far more powerful than the hope for subsidized grain.

The census reveals much about ordinary life in Renaissance Rome, providing an important snapshot of the city's people, their origins, their living arrangements, and their occupations.[13] It divided the city into fourteen districts (*rioni*), as shown in the map (on p. xviii, facing p. 1), each with a distinct character, banners, traditions, and pride. The most densely populated areas were in Campo Marzio (IV), Ponte (V), Parione (VI), Regola (VII), and S. Eustachio (VIII), in the U-shape formed by a bend in the Tiber River, and those rioni directly on the opposite riverbank, Trastevere (XIII) and Borgo (XIV), the location of the Vatican.

The census recorded 9,285 separate households containing a total of 55,035 mouths to feed or bodies to tax. The actual number of residents may have been twice that, with the uncounted no doubt less well-off and stable than the included. People with less secure employment, including most women and many younger men, were most likely to be enumerated without an occupation being listed. In short, numbers and percentages are minimums, with a statistical bias against the inclusion of marginal people. A most startling and important fact leaps from the data: Women headed 2,220 of the households, nearly one in four, with 448 women heads, about one-fifth, recorded as living alone. A few of these singles were listed as widows, and significantly more as laundresses and courtesans; however, most were identified by place of origin rather than occupation. The heaviest concentrations of single women, 8 to 9 percent of total households, were in Borgo, Regola, and S. Eustachio, followed by Ponte and Campo Marzio at 5 to 6 percent. These districts were within easy walking distance of the residences of the pope, the cardinals, and other high clerics whose licentious behavior many of Rome's shocked visitors so loudly denounced. Another 615 female-headed households included only one additional person; here, too, the statistical profile suggests the accuracy of what observers reported: women involved in serving men, some explicitly in the sex trade and others noted as laundresses, barmaids, or housekeepers, abounded everywhere along the Tiber. Some of these female-headed households recorded a mother and child, but others were of the kind described by the essayist Montaigne (Document 15) and more intimately by the artist Benvenuto Cellini (Document 18): a courtesan (prostitute, usually sought after as well for her artistic ability) and her maidservant.

Most female-headed households record place of origin, and hundreds of them are noted as Spanish, German, French, Corsican, Slavic, and Greek. These women lived in clusters, as did their sisters from the Italian peninsula: Florentines, Venetians, Neapolitans, Milanese, Bolognese, Sicilians, and Sienese, roughly in that numerical order. Women identified specifically as Roman outnumber those of any other label, but the total number of foreigners, with or without including women from the Italian peninsula, is considerably greater.

How did all these independent women get by in Renaissance Rome? Cellini's autobiographical account and Francisco Delicado's fictional tale (Document 17) provide some spicy details about life on Rome's streets and behind its crowded portals. The hard facts from the census are clear, showing the extraordinary presence in Campo Marzio of nearly 13.9 percent of all households headed by a woman and one companion, followed by 10 percent in Borgo and more than 8 percent in Ponte and Regola. Three-person female-headed households were also prominent in Campo Marzio, above 10 percent, but the pattern ceases to exist in all other districts and in households above this size. Still, with close to one-quarter of all households headed by a female, Rome was unique among the world's cities for the proportion of its women who lived on their own.[14] The census lists only a few dozen among the 2,220 female heads as courtesans or with the derogatory term *puttane* (sometimes scribbled in the margin), preferring to identify them by place of origin. In this sense they might be classified among the excluded of Rome's people, but when the hard realities of Renaissance life are put together with what is known from literary and other sources (Documents 17 and

18), it becomes clear that they constituted a major part of Rome's population, serving men's needs and desires in one way or another. This is not to say that they were all sex workers, or that they were sex workers and nothing else, only that their lives were heavily taken up with service to men.

The Excluded

Pilgrims and other visitors to Rome commented upon the prominent yet deeply compromised place of its Jewish community. Jews had begun migrating to the city as early as the second century BCE, and despite serious restrictions and setbacks, by the year 1000 CE Roman Jews experienced something of a golden age.[15] The papacy generally defended Jews from the most radical secular attempts to deny them freedom of worship and to seize their property without legal due process. Trials and tribulations ranging from inquisitorial prosecution to ritual stoning followed over the centuries, increasingly after 1300, but with the ascension of Francesco della Rovere as Pope Sixtus IV in 1471, formal restrictions on Jewish business activity and property-holding eased considerably. By 1492, when Spain expelled all its Jews, a flourishing Roman Jewish community, including some wealthy bankers and merchants, felt sufficiently threatened with being inundated by coreligionist immigrants that they attempted to bribe Spanish Pope Alexander VI to refuse residency permits to the refugees. Instead, the pope placed a residency tax on the existing Jewish population, while continuing to draw on the community for its gifted medical practitioners, musicians, and scholars.[16]

Francisco Delicado, author of *La Lozana Andaluza* (Document 17), recounts the daily life of Rome's less fortunate Jews. Delicado may have been among those exiled by Spain in 1492, which would explain how he could have known so much and written with such poignancy.[17] Reports of degradation also appear in English visitor Anthony Munday's account of Jews stripped naked and forced to race from the Porta del Popolo to the Capitoline for the enjoyment of spectators celebrating Mardi Gras (Document 14). The profound anti-Semitism behind such merriment is also revealed in remarks attacking Alfonso de Valdès (Document 20) by Baldassare (Baltasar) Castiglione, known primarily for his book of etiquette, *The Courtier*, but important in the present context for his unfounded accusation that Jews were somehow responsible for the 1527 sack of Rome.

The history of Renaissance Rome's Jews drew to its sorry conclusion with Pope Paul IV's (r. 1555–1559) issuance in 1555 of a decree

(Document 8), formally titled a *bulla* (bull, named for the metal seal at the bottom of the proclamation). Among other provisions, it forced all Jews in papal territories to live in ghettos and restricted their economic activities with Christians to the sale of used clothing, thus barring them from all but the lowliest means of earning a living. As to the city of Rome, the bull only confirmed centuries-old realities, documented two decades earlier in the 1526–1527 census: Of the 318 households listed as headed by Jews containing a total of 1,515 souls, all but a dozen were located in the core community, essentially a self-created ghetto around the synagogue and within close walking distance of papal economic activity, packed between the ruins of the ancient Portico di Ottavia and along the Tiber to Hadrian's Bridge leading to Castel Sant' Angelo. Used clothes peddlers and junk sellers outnumbered all other occupations, followed by shoemakers, butchers, and tailors. There were a few physicians, musicians, and philosophers, some of whom prudently chose not to list their professions in an official census document that might be used for nefarious purposes.

THE ECONOMICS OF RENAISSANCE ROME (LEGITIMATE AND NOT)

Rather than production, lavish consumption at the apex, dominated by the needs and desires of the church, formed the basis of Renaissance Rome's local economy. Approximately 7,500 men and women, amounting to about 15 percent of Rome's enumerated population, were directly connected to church institutions, but their effect as consumers was far greater. A dinner party hosted by papal banker Agostino Chigi for Pope Leo X and his entourage provides a memorable example. On earlier occasions, several cardinals had made a habit of stealing silver serving vessels by hiding them under their robes, so for this particular feast Chigi ordered gold plates for everyone, but insisted that they be tossed into the Tiber River after each serving. Guests loved this exquisite wastefulness, little knowing that the clever banker's servants had placed fishing nets in the river earlier that day, from which he recovered his precious goods early the next morning.[18]

More ordinary yet equally telling facts come from municipal records. According to the 1526–1527 census, Pope Clement VII's (r. 1523–1534) resident staff tallied at an even 700. Another 76 cardinals and bishops headed households containing a total of 4,406 mouths to feed, ranging from the 306 people who served Cardinal Alessandro Farnese (future

Pope Paul III, r. 1534–1549) to the one additional person under the roof of humble Archbishop of Rosana. Another 145 households, with a total of 978 residents, were headed by less august clerical persons who lived outside a specifically designated church or monastery, some with titles such as abbot, abbess, chaplain, monsignor, priest, monk, and nun. Other churchmen were listed with occupational designations such as notary and auditor (judge). They served at the Apostolic Tribunal of the Sacred Roman Rota, named *rota* (wheel) starting in the fourteenth century for the rounded benches used at this highest appellate court. Powerful Christian Rome was also known throughout Europe for the charity it offered to visitors, a reputation well-deserved judging by the census listing of seventeen hospitals giving care gratis to some 972 people, including the massive papal operation at Santo Spirito with an estimated 500 residents. Another 575 people made their homes within the city's eighty-five churches, while its fifty-one monasteries housed a reported 1,127 men and women. Altogether, then, among the 55,035 residents counted in Rome for the 1526–1527 census, more than 7,500 were directly connected with the work of the church in a formal institutional sense.

Secular workers in what today might broadly be called the service sector tended to the needs of all these churchmen and women, along with the members of their households. Notable for their absence in the census are significant numbers of artisans or other laborers typically found in an economy based on production. Instead, the listings show more than a hundred tavern keepers, hosts, and hostesses, outnumbered only by tailors, shoemakers, bakers, barbers, and delicatessen workers, in that order. The city's endless building needs are reflected in substantial numbers of male bricklayers, carpenters, and metal workers, while among women sixty-six are identified as laundresses and twenty-nine as courtesans. From two to four dozen entries list male booksellers, copyists, sword makers, artists, medical doctors (twelve surgeons and six physicians), and jewelers. Transportation needs were met by many tens of mule drivers, haulers, carriage drivers, and water-carriers, while provisioning involved similar numbers of butchers, spice and wine dealers, fishmongers, and sellers of fruits and vegetables. Smaller but still significant numbers of specialists in furs, silks, perfumes, and haberdashery also appear on the census lists, a clear indication of the upper echelon's penchant for public ostentation.[19]

Alongside the legitimate economy were a considerable number of Renaissance Romans engaged in criminal activities, including usury, fraud, graft, robbery, and violent street crime. The Eternal City was accurately reputed to be a dangerous place to live or to visit, and the risks were nothing new, as may be surmised from Juvenal's *Satire 3*, written around the year 112 CE:

> This is not all you must fear. Shut up your house or your store,
> Bolts and padlocks and bars will never keep out all the burglars,
> Or a holdup man will do you in with a switch blade.
> If the guards are strong over Pontine marshes and pinewoods
> Near Volturno, the scum of the swamps and the filth of the forest
> Swirl into Rome, the great sewer, their sanctuary, their haven.[20]

The dangers had not diminished much by the late eighteenth century, when one of the city's most illustrious literary visitors, Johann Wolfgang von Goethe, reported that "what strikes any foreigner are the murders which happen almost every day. In our quarter alone, there have been four in the last three weeks. . . . [In one case the] assailant, with whom [the victim] had got into a scuffle, stabbed him twenty times, and when the guards arrived, the villain stabbed himself. This is not the fashion here [in Rome]. Usually, the murderer takes sanctuary in a church, and that is the end of that."[21] Some killings served no clear economic purpose and were the outcome of prideful disputes among elite men who resorted all too easily to their swords—a reality conveyed in the writings of the sculptor Cellini (Document 18) and the biography of the painter Michelangelo Merisi da Caravaggio, best known simply as Caravaggio (Document 10). But the overall climate of violence on the streets of Rome, where strangers might be knifed to death for a petty *quattrino* (a coin worth four pennies) or a former business associate turned enemy might be dispatched with a fatal clubbing, was a widely understood and accepted reality of daily life in the Renaissance.

CIVIC REBIRTH DEFEATED

When historians expanded the definition of the Renaissance to include not only artistic developments but also other areas of human creativity, especially civic governance, they greatly enhanced its meaning and scope. As previously discussed, so doing ultimately raised fundamental questions about the poor, women, and other groups for whom there was no rebirth or golden age. Furthermore, there is the thorny issue of how the story of Renaissance Rome challenges historians' assertion of a causal relationship between Renaissance Florence's inclusive, proto-democratic political fabric and its collective artistic genius. Rome experienced autocratic papal government triumphant over participatory civic institutions, but also nurtured an age of artistic creativity. One answer may be that both representative and totalitarian political systems may support an era such as the Renaissance, although by very different paths.

Historians observe that civic-minded early Renaissance Romans consciously sought future greatness for the Eternal City by invoking the glories of its past. They recalled the first two centuries of the empire, known as the Pax Romana, as a time when Rome's peaceful rule extended from Britannia to Mesopotamia. Then came the official legalization of Christian worship under Emperor Constantine (313), followed two centuries later by the invasions of so-called barbarians, initiating a millennium of decline. The low point came in 1309 when the papacy relocated to the southern French city of Avignon. No longer the center of Western Christendom, the city fell victim to decades of internal strife. Moreover, the power of the state was no longer being challenged by the power of the church. Rome's barony, freed from papal dominance, cut loose in a savage and seemingly endless civil war between allies of the tightly knit Orsini and Colonna families. Each faction brought the wealth and manpower of its enormous country estates to the streets of central Rome, turning ancient ruins into crude fortifications and erecting barricades aimed more at looting than at a rational effort to seize power.

Into this chaos came Cola di Rienzo, first as leader of a coup d'état in 1347, then as tribune (mayor, dictator) of Rome, and then in a brief return to power in 1354 as papal senator. One modern historian hails Cola di Rienzo as the founder of the Renaissance; others portray him as a forerunner of the popular hero of Italy's unification (1860–1871), Giuseppe Garibaldi, and of its foremost villain, twentieth-century Fascist dictator Benito Mussolini. Cola explicitly invoked the deeds of Julius Caesar (assassinated 44 BCE) as he attempted to singlehandedly forge a communal government for Rome such as existed in many northern Italian cities at this time, but for which there was absolutely no basis in Rome's historical evolution. To these impossible tasks Cola added a vision of a unified state embracing the entire peninsula and promptly attempted to implement his lofty ideal by conferring Roman citizenship on all "Italians." Finally, he proclaimed the beginning of the age of the Holy Ghost on earth, one based on the mystical beliefs of proponents of absolute Franciscan poverty known as the Fraticelli, who had been declared to be heretical by Pope Boniface VIII (r. 1294–1303) in 1296. All these dreams came to a gruesome end in October 1354 when the powerful Colonna family encouraged a popular riot during which the mob killed Cola di Rienzo and publically desecrated his body.[22]

The next hundred years, marked by the permanent return to Rome of the papacy in 1377, witnessed a series of attempts to establish a strong civilian government independent of papal authority. These efforts failed utterly, in sharp contrast to the experience of Italian cities to the north, such as Florence and Siena. In Rome there would be no rebirth of secular authority, no return to the glory of the ancient empire, and consequently no unification of the Italian peninsula. The contrast between Rome and its sister cities to the north suggests that the demise of secular governance may have been the necessary price of, or at least the pathway to, the unified vision of papal grandeur that came to be reflected in the city's streets, palaces, and churches—the Renaissance Rome whose art and architectural magnificence visitors may still see there today. Certainly a pope set on bringing glory to his reign by commissioning permanent artistic monuments no longer had to be concerned with the petty dictates of local politicians. Here is a historical conundrum worth considering, even if it cannot be resolved with certainty. Italian city-states with secular and participatory governance—Florence being the exemplar—nurtured the great cultural achievements known as the Renaissance just as similar accomplishments flourished in authoritarian papal Rome. The vast differences between these cities beg the question of the relevance of political systems to how the Renaissance is defined and assessed.

If any single date can be assigned as the terminus for meaningful secular government in Rome, a good choice is 1453, the year of the execution of Stefano Porcaro, a local political leader less charismatic than Cola di Rienzo but with considerably greater skills in statecraft. (See Document 2.) His talents were no match for the rising power of Pope Nicholas V, in whose reign the papacy established political dominion over Rome that continued until Italy's complete unification in 1870, interrupted only temporarily by Napoleon I's direct rule from 1805 to 1814. Insider details about Porcaro's fate come from Stefano Infessura, the uncompromisingly antipapal diarist who served as secretary to the Roman Senate for many years, a scribe always ready to do the bidding of his patrons in the Colonna family:

> On the 9th of January, a Tuesday, Messer Stefano Porcaro was hanged in Castel [Sant' Angelo] in the tower to the right, on the merlons, and I saw him dressed in a black vest and black *pennere* hose, that man who loved the good and the liberty of Rome. He saw himself banished from Rome without cause; wishing for this reason to liberate his country from

servitude, he gave his own life, as well as his own body. Some say he was interred in Santa Maria and others say he was thrown in the river.[23]

A diametrically opposite account may be found in Ludwig Pastor's highly engaging classic, *History of the Popes.* To this pro-papal historian, Porcaro was an ungrateful and duplicitous revolutionary guilty of high treason against the legitimate government of Pope Nicholas V. The pope initially tried to appease Porcaro with a far-away governorship, then with an ambassadorship, and finally with a gentle exile in Bologna supported with an annual pension of three hundred ducats. Porcaro escaped even this mild punishment and returned hastily to Rome, where he gathered a small group of plotters who intended to set the Vatican Palace on fire and then surprise the pope and assembled cardinals at high mass on the Feast of the Epiphany. The plan was to kill as many of them as necessary before seizing Castel Sant' Angelo and taking over the Campidoglio, where Porcaro would be declared tribune of a liberated Roman republic.

As events turned out, tiredness overtook Porcaro and betrayals followed. Porcaro ingloriously attempted to hide in a chest beneath a woman's skirts, and finally he fully confessed, after which he was summarily executed. Pastor closes his treatment of Porcaro's failed plot with an assessment that directly links the glories of the Renaissance to the suppression of ancient Rome's legacy: "The terrible event exercised a most injurious influence on the excitable and impressionable nature of the Pope . . . from the moment that the phantom of the ancient Republic arose, threatening destruction to his life, his authority, and all his magnificent undertakings on behalf of art and learning, his peace of mind was gone. He became melancholy, reserved, and inaccessible."[24]

For the next several centuries, until the 1860s and the unification of Italy, the papacy had nothing to fear internally in the arena of city governance. Powerful baronial families from the countryside, such as the Colonna, might still ally against the papacy and even field an army to imperil its safety, as Pope Clement VII would learn the hard way, but that was essentially an external matter. Within the city, a compliant local government continued to function nominally but without power. Petty bureaucrats willingly obeyed dictates from the Vatican, whether to make way for a new processional avenue by demolishing humble homes or to enforce only laxly the city's regulations against public display. With the exception of the especially sensitive Clement VII during the years 1527 to 1532, the sixteenth-century papacy allowed the posting of satiric political verses as a safety valve for hostile public opinion. These came to be known as *pasquinades* (Document 7), named after the Hellenistic

statue dubbed Pasquino upon which the writings were anonymously placed at night (Figure 4). This form of protest amounted to no more than lighthearted literary sport, a tradition that continues to the present day, albeit with less literary flair.[25]

Rome's streets belonged to the popes, who would play, parade, build, and beautify them as their fancies dictated, often with little regard for cost or public opinion. Probably no pope exceeded Leo X, whose lavish expenditures precipitated the financial crisis behind the Protestant Reformation. For his efforts, he even received a favorable ditty pasted to Pasquino:

> I used to be an exile, but I'm back in Leo's reign
> So burn your midnight oil, boys, and follow in my train;
> For no one leaves my Leo without a handsome gain;
> Bards will sing for prizes, and they'll not sing in vain.[26]

The Roman people loved spectacle. They would obey the pope, profit where possible, and enjoy life to the fullest, at least according to the observers who flocked to the city. A medical expert attempting to diagnose why Rome's women were especially fertile and its men suffered bloated heads and cirrhosis of the liver agreed, ascribing both conditions to the good life prized above all else by Romans rich and poor (Document 9).

THE SACK OF ROME

Successful as Renaissance popes were in taming Rome's civic political spirit, they ultimately failed to defend their city and their empire against outside forces competing for the governance of Western Christendom. The Protestant Reformation marked a political as well as a spiritual disaster for the papacy, even in the regions of Europe that remained Catholic. The sack of Rome in 1527 revealed fundamental flaws in the unity of church and state championed by the papacy. The Papal State

---

Opposite: **Figure 4.** *Statue of Pasquino*
The third-century BCE Hellenistic statue of Pasquino, which was unearthed in the Parione district in the fifteenth century and placed just outside Piazza Navona, a popular gathering place. Upon this statue, Renaissance satirists posted poetic barbs against the pope and other powerful Romans, which came to be known as *pasquinades*. Today, the statue serves a similar purpose, as people post diatribes against contemporary political leaders.

had never been truly powerful in a strictly military sense and had always depended on a delicate web of shrewd diplomacy propped upon a foundation of spiritual superiority. The latter, of course, was hard to claim in the face of realities to be seen by all on Rome's streets and inner courtyards, but pretenses had their uses. For centuries the façade of the Eternal City as Western Christendom's crown jewel had served the needs of Europe's contesting rulers, who were stalemated in an unending battle to maintain a balance of power. In the sixteenth century the balance shifted due to the infusion of New World wealth into Spain and the ascendancy of France as a unified state. These nations ultimately remained Catholic, but they no longer needed a politically independent papacy. The Germanic areas of the Holy Roman Empire turned heavily toward Protestantism, leaving Rome and its popes with no possible way to carry on as an independent secular power. Balance of power issues remained for Europe as a whole, but after 1527 the papacy rapidly became a bit player.

As a large contingent of troops invaded the Italian peninsula in the spring of that year, pressures dating back to Pope Gregory VII's (1073–1085) humiliation of the Holy Roman emperor Henry IV during the investiture controversy exploded. The immediate military campaign had begun in 1521 when an alliance of England, the Holy Roman Empire, and the papacy against France reached a stalemate in Flanders and the Netherlands. The field of battle shifted to northern Italy, where France, now joined by Venice, had territorial pretensions. The French consistently lost a series of skirmishes in Lombardy over the next several years, but failure did not deter King Francis I (r. 1515–1547). He personally led an attack on Milan in the spring of 1525 that was initially successful, only to undergo a disastrous defeat and the king's capture at the battle of Pavia shortly thereafter. While in captivity, King Francis signed an agreement renouncing all territorial ambitions in Flanders and Italy, which he broke once Pope Clement VII released him. The pope feared the growing influence of Holy Roman Emperor Charles V (r. 1519–1556), even though he desperately needed the emperor's political and military strength for the looming conflict with German Lutherans. Displaying his uncanny knack for allying with the losing side in any fight, Clement VII shifted his support to the French. In retaliation, Charles V authorized an invasion of Italy for the spring of 1527, presumably to counter expected French military activities and as a warning to the pope.

Charles V placed Charles III, Duke of Bourbon (1490–1527), in command of this army. The duke had switched sides, betraying his former sovereign Francis I over a dispute about confiscated territories that the duke thought he had inherited through his wife. Both Emperor Charles V and Duke Charles III had been involved in an earlier secret plot, which also included King Henry VIII of England, to conquer France and divide it among the three of them, but the bold plan failed to materialize. Duke Charles III then had fled to Italy, where he had become a principal commander of troops in opposition to Francis I, and where he had led the victors in the decisive battle of Pavia at which Francis I had been taken prisoner.

The core of Duke Charles III's latest and last army included some six thousand Spanish troops and approximately fourteen thousand German mercenaries, many of them Lutherans. They were augmented by several contingents of armed men bent on plunder, led by professional soldiers of fortune known in Italy as *condottieri*, who sold themselves to the highest bidder in Italy's endless civil wars. This amounted to a total of about thirty-four thousand troops. While Emperor Charles V had authorized the army, he had failed to provide it with provisions and with money to pay the troops. Charles III did what he could to hold his forces together, promising them opportunities to loot and pillage. After his soldiers dispatched the opposing French forces in several engagements and still found themselves with empty bellies and no cash, they forced Charles III to lead them toward Rome, renowned as a place of fabulous wealth. By this point Pope Clement VII had reached a new agreement with Emperor Charles V, but that alliance of convenience meant nothing as the troops eagerly pressed ahead, looting along the way and hungry for the big prize. They reached Rome's western walls by May 5 and began an assault the next morning. Charles III, easy to spot in his flowing white cloak, was fatally shot (Cellini and his boys claimed the marksmanship for that one),[27] leaving his troops without leadership (Document 18). The invaders easily breached the city's walls and went on a rampage in search of hidden treasure, pausing only to rape, maul, and ridicule both lay and clerical men and women (Document 16).

Whether Rome ever fully recovered from this profound political miscalculation by the pope is widely disputed. When this focus is on rebuilding efforts and the visible splendors of the late Renaissance and Baroque periods, the answer is "yes." When Rome is taken as leader and lynchpin of the revitalization achieved by the Catholic Reformation, with its consolidation of power throughout southern Europe, in much of central Europe, and eventually in France, the answer is also "yes." But when one asks whether Rome survived as the center of Western civilization and the global capital of Christendom, the answer is "no."

Rome after 1527 was still a wondrous place to visit, but it was no longer the heart and soul of the Christian West.

WESTERN CHRISTENDOM SUNDERED

The late Renaissance and the early Reformation eras occupy the same chronological span—the sixteenth century—and their histories are deeply entwined, especially in Rome. On January 3, 1521, Pope Leo X took sufficient notice of Martin Luther's various acts of defiance to issue a bull declaring the recalcitrant monk to be a heretic. This was in essence an individual condemnation made on religious grounds. But from the outset, the fate of Martin Luther and his followers, along with the destinies of fellow Protestants of all denominations, depended less on theological dialogues than on political dynamics. Leo X died the same year that he excommunicated Luther for heresy; after an eighteen-month interregnum he was replaced by his cousin, Giulio de' Medici, who took the name Clement VII. This pope's lack of political acuity, as already described, contributed greatly to the disastrous sack of Rome in 1527, as acknowledged by his generally supportive fellow Florentine, Luigi Guicciardini (Document 16). Pope Clement VII turned out to be no more successful in his dealings with the theological challenges raised by Protestant dissenters to the north. The papacy also ignored or actively suppressed the impulses of deep spirituality that once had flourished on Rome's streets in the lives of holy women such as Catherine of Siena (Document 3) and Francesca Romana (Document 4). Instead, it moved forward in imperial style with the construction of the magnificent and expensive basilica of St. Peter's, launched on Julius II's initiative in 1506 and finally dedicated in 1626, at the close of the Renaissance proper.[28]

Additionally, Clement VII's refusal to sanction English King Henry VIII's divorce from Catherine of Aragon, whatever the merits of the case on legal grounds, proved to be a political disaster. It triggered a chain of events that permanently destabilized the balance of power in continental Europe upon which the papacy's secular power always had depended. The wars of religion ensued, lasting officially until the treaties known collectively as the Peace of Westphalia in 1648. The result was a dismantled Holy Roman Empire and a truncated territory for the Papal States, the latter hardly more than a dependency of Spain and holding dominion only at the mercy of France. The era of the nation-state had arrived, with England, France, and Spain leading the way. The Papal State was a weak historical anachronism, not a nation.

Religious dissent went hand in hand with political fragmentation. From the outset, leading Catholic intellectuals who had lived in Rome and had seen the ostentatious corruption displayed on its streets excoriated the papacy for its unchristian behavior. Alfonso de Valdès (Document 20) died while still professing loyalty to Rome, as did his twin brother a few years later, but the works of both authors raised profound doubts about church dogma and nurtured outright heresy. Similarly, Desiderius Erasmus (Document 21) remained within the Catholic fold, but his *Praise of Folly*, to this day a staple in college curricula, left no doubt about his disdain for much Catholic doctrine and practice.[29] Martin Luther took a different path, breaking completely with Rome, although it might be said that Rome broke with him (Document 22). Either way, his experience in the Eternal City essentially caused him to concur with his fellow thinkers who died as Catholics.

In 1542, a quarter-century after Luther first posted his Ninety-Five Theses criticizing the church in Wittenberg, Germany, Pope Paul III issued *Licet ab initio*, the bull that instituted the Roman Inquisition. Its purpose was to stamp out all dissent from Catholic doctrine. Over the next three decades, the influence of this body, formally known as the Supreme Sacred Congregation of the Roman and Universal Inquisition, extended rapidly throughout the Italian peninsula and beyond to geographically separate locations including Malta and Avignon. The city of Rome, once known for welcoming strangers—whatever their purposes and circumstances—now became wary of visitors who might bear the taint of heresy. From across the Alps came Lutherans, as all denominations of Protestants were labeled; from the kingdom of Naples came followers of Juan de Valdès who had carried the logic of his queries beyond the limits of his personal Catholic orthodoxy; from Venice came heretics carrying their infectious books; and from within the church itself emerged priests and monks with restless and unstable minds. The Roman Inquisition generally followed well-established judicial practices dating back to the Middle Ages, including admirable legal protections for the accused. Overall, it was less harsh in its treatment of suspects than its Spanish and Portuguese counterparts, which directed their efforts primarily against Moriscos (converts from Islam) and Morranos (secret Jews). The objective of saving souls, explicitly stated in all Roman inquisitorial manuals, would have been an oxymoron in determining appropriate punishment for false converts to Christianity, since only the souls of true Christians could be saved under any circumstances.[30]

The Roman Inquisition is best known for its condemnation in 1633 of Galileo Galilei as "vehemently suspected of heresy," a notch below the degree of culpability that could have sent him to the stake. Like most of the 50,000 to 75,000 men and women brought before Rome's tribunals, Galileo did not pay with his life. Still, at least 1,200 people did, including the friar Giordano Bruno (Document 23), a philosopher and mathematician whose dark statue today looms over the bustling Campo dei Fiori square, tucked between the central Regola and Parione rioni, where he was burned at the stake.[31] Most tourists strolling by today think the somber pose must represent some austere saint, but for Romans in the know, the statue is an emblem of the triumph of civic authority over the papacy that came with Italy's unification in 1860, its military conquest of Rome in 1870, and the plebiscite that ended 1,500 years of papal "occupation" in favor of annexation to the secular nation of Italy.

The quixotic statue of Giordano Bruno in Campo dei Fiori symbolizes the ultimate triumph of political and intellectual freedom over the tyranny of religious intolerance. Protection of individual liberty of expression, whether on matters related to earth or to heaven, did not exist during the Renaissance. But the freedoms we enjoy today, in America and throughout the democratic world, are the direct legacy of positions forged and contests waged at that time.[32] As noted throughout this introduction, the Renaissance struggle for political domination, with its origins in the medieval investiture controversy,[33] pitted papal against secular rulers. The later fight by Cola di Rienzo for control over the city of Rome in the mid-fourteenth century ended in victory for the papacy, but its triumph did not last. In the sixteenth century and beyond, the Protestant and Catholic Reformations initiated a renewed and more virulent contest that extended throughout Europe and then across the entire globe. The sundering of Western Christendom, established politically only after a century of religious wars, paved the way for the eventual separation of church and state, expressed so forcefully in the First Amendment to the Constitution of the United States. This separation, arguably, provides the only historically proven basis for a society that protects individual liberty of thought and action. Though not perfect, our world owes much to the successes and failures of our Renaissance forebears.

Along with being an era of extraordinary artistic and literary achievement, the Renaissance should be understood to include its lesser-known struggle for survival by the masses. Much work is yet to be done as historians of the next generation seek to gain an even deeper and more varied portrait of this era in Rome and beyond. Rome's story is rich in the details of daily lives filled with the excitement of festivals and the enjoyment of worldly pleasures great and small. Whether other Europeans experienced the Renaissance in similar ways remains an open question.

NOTES

[1]Ingrid D. Rowland, *The Culture of the High Renaissance: Ancients and Moderns in Sixteenth-Century Rome* (Cambridge, U.K.: Cambridge University Press, 1998), 1–12, nicely emphasizes the centrality of Rome as a physical space for humanism. The documents in the present volume do not address the subject of Renaissance humanism, which deserves a separate study that would necessary focus well beyond Rome as a place. The bibliography includes suggestions for further reading on this subject.

[2]Cristina Mazzoni, *She-Wolf: The Story of a Roman Icon* (Cambridge, U.K.: Cambridge University Press, 2010), 2–3, 51–55.

[3]Andreas Rehberg and Anna Modigliani, eds., *Cola di Rienzo e il Comune di Roma*, 2 vols. (Rome: Roma nel Rinascimento, 2004), provides the latest interpretative material and related documents.

[4]Dante Alighieri, *The Inferno*, trans. John Ciardi (New York: Penguin, 1954), Canto XVIII, ll, 25–33.

[5]Georgina Masson, *Courtesans of the Italian Renaissance* (New York: St. Martin's Press, 1975), provides a well-documented positive assessment of the courtesans at the top of the sex-trade pyramid.

[6]Dante Alighieri, *The Purgatorio*, trans. John Ciardi (New York: Penguin, 1957), Canto XXXII, ll. 100–102.

[7]Fabrizio Winspeare, *La Congiura dei Cardianli contro Leone X* (Florence: Olschki, 1957), cited in Rowland, *Culture of the High Renaissance*, 240.

[8]Joan Kelly Gadol, "Did Women Have a Renaissance?" in Renate Bridenthal and Claudia Koonz, eds., *Becoming Visible: Women in European History* (Boston: Houghton Mifflin, 1977), 139–66.

[9]John Jeffries Martin, ed., *The Renaissance: Italy and Abroad* (London and New York: Routledge, 2003), 1–19, shapes this brief overview of the word *Renaissance*.

[10]Thomas F. X. Noble, "Rome and the Romans in the Medieval Mind: Empathy and Antipathy," in Karl F. Morrison and Rudolph M. Bell, eds., *Experiments in Empathy: The Middle Ages* (Turnhout, Belg.: Brepols, forthcoming).

[11]Hugh Shankland, ed. and trans., *The Prettiest Love Letters in the World: Letters between Lucrezia Borgia and Pietro Bembo 1503–1519* (Boston: David R. Godine, 1985), 23.

[12]Rowland, *Culture of the High Renaissance*, 143, is powerful in her positive assessment.

[13]Egmont Lee, ed., *Habitatores in Urbe: The Population of Renaissance Rome* (Rome: Università degli Studi di Roma, 2006), provides a thorough analysis of the census and also PDF files with indexes to the actual census entries, from which I compiled the statistics that follow on households by gender, origin, and occupation.

[14]See Rudolph M. Bell and Virginia Yans, *Women on Their Own: Interdisciplinary Perspectives on Being Single* (New Brunswick, N.J.: Rutgers University Press, 2008), for a comparative perspective extending to the contemporary West. See Rowland, *Culture of the High Renaissance*, 26 and 261 n. 43 on Roman women and property holding and 91 on sartorial distinctions between courtesans and proper Roman matrons.

[15]Robert Bonfil, *Jewish Life in Renaissance Italy*, trans. Anthony Oldcorn (Berkeley: University of California Press, 1994), 95.

[16]Kenneth Stow, *Theater of Acculturation: The Roman Ghetto in the Sixteenth Century* (Seattle: University of Washington Press, 2001), 13–22; Attilio Milano, *Il Ghetto di Roma* (Rome: Carucci, 1988), 53–65.

[17]Bruno Damiani, *Francisco Delicado* (New York: Twayne Publishers, 1974), 13–15.

[18]Rowland, *Culture of the High Renaissance*, 242. See Giuseppe Cugnoni, *Agostino Chigi il Magnifico* (Rome: Istituto di Studi Romani, Archivio della Reale Società Romana di Storia Patria, 1878).

[19]Space precludes full discussion of Rome's economy, but I wish to indicate the sort of detailed work that is possible for this section by citing Angela Lanconelli, "Il Commercio del Pesce a Roma nel Tardo Medioevo," in Anna Esposito and Luciano Palermo, eds.,

Economia e Società a Roma tra Medioevo e Rinascimento: Studi Dedicati ad Arnold Esch (Rome: Viella, 2005), 181–203.

[20]Rolfe Humphries, trans., *The Satires of Juvenal* (Bloomington: Indiana University Press, 1958), Satire 3, ll. 303–8.

[21]Johann Wolfgang von Goethe, *Italian Journey (1786–1788)*, trans. W. H. Auden and Elizabeth Mayer (New York: Pantheon Books, 1962), 132.

[22]John Wright, trans. and ed., *The Life of Cola di Rienzo* (Toronto: Pontifical Institute of Mediaeval Studies, 1975), 15–20.

[23]Oreste Tommasini, ed., *Diario della Città di Roma di Stefano Infessura* (Rome: Forzani, 1890), 54.

[24]Ludwig Pastor, *The History of the Popes*, ed. and trans. Frederick Ignatius Antrobus II (London: Kegan Paul, 1899), 238 for the quotation and 220–39 more generally.

[25]Valerio Marucci, Antonio Marzo, and Angelo Romano, eds., *Pasquinate Romane del Cinquecento*, 2 vols (Rome: Salerno, 1983), ix–xxv for the historical context.

[26]Rowland, *Culture of the High Renaissance*, 211, cites Julia Hauig Gaisser, "The Rise and Fall of Göritz's Feasts," *Renaissance Quarterly* 48 (1995): 41.

[27]John Addington Symonds, trans., *The Autobiography of Benvenuto Cellini* (New York: Garden City, 1927), 64–65.

[28]Thomas Dandelet, "Searching for the New Constantine: Early Modern Rome as a Spanish Imperial City," in Gary B. Cohen and Franz A. J. Szabo, eds., *Embodiments of Power: Building Baroque Cities in Europe* (New York: Berghahn Books, 2008), 191–202, succinctly draws out the political implications of Rome's architectural projects.

[29]See Léon-E. Halkin, *Erasmus: A Critical Biography*, trans. John Tonkin (Oxford, U.K.: Blackwell, 1987), 64–74.

[30]Christopher F. Black, *The Italian Inquisition* (New Haven, Conn., and London: Yale University Press), 1–18, on the establishment of the Roman Inquisition. Jane K. Wickersham, *Rituals of Prosecution: The Roman Inquisition and the Prosecution of Philo-Protestants in Sixteenth-Century Italy* (Toronto: University of Toronto Press, 2012), considers in depth the goals and methods of Roman inquisitors and the manuals written to guide them.

[31]Karen Silvia de León-Jones, *Giordano Bruno and the Kabbalah: Prophets, Magicians, and Rabbis* (New Haven, Conn.: Yale University Press, 1997), 3, for Brunomania. Ingrid D. Rowland, *Giordano Bruno: Philosopher/Heretic* (Chicago: University of Chicago Press, 2009), is the best choice for an English-language biography.

[32]Brad Gregory, *The Unintended Reformation: How a Religious Revolution Secularized Society* (New Haven, Conn.: Yale University Press, 2012), provides a rich exploration of this theme.

[33]Maureen C. Miller, *Power and the Holy in the Age of the Investiture Conflict: A Brief History with Documents* (Boston: Bedford/St. Martin's, 2005).

The Documents

1

Renaissance Beginnings

1

GIOVANNI BOCCACCIO

The Decameron

ca. 1350–1352

In 1348 an epidemic of bubonic plague known as the Black Death ravished Florence and much of the Italian peninsula, eventually bringing death to as many as one in every three people. In defiant response, Florentine diplomat, businessman, and prolific writer Giovanni Boccaccio (1313–1375) penned one hundred novellas collectively titled The Decameron. *In the preface to this wickedly funny collection, he stated his intention to combat the ensuing sense of depression felt by his readers, especially women. No one escaped Boccaccio's satiric barbs: not his hero Dante, homosexuals, haughty intellectuals and professors, dishonest judges, jealous husbands, false friends, men past their sexual prime, greedy in-laws, and especially those who had taken religious vows, whatever their gender or rank. The story that follows—the second told on the first day of an imaginary ten-day journey by seven ladies and three of their suitors—uses the device of a Jewish subject to criticize Rome's clerics for their corruption of Christian values. This universal observation about the clergy, present since the beginning of the Renaissance in the fourteenth century, remained vibrant centuries later, as seen in Martin Luther's* Table Talk *(Document 22). Boccaccio's tale also provides a glimpse of Rome's thriving Jewish community.*

Giovanni Boccaccio, *The Decameron* (London: Navarre Society Limited, 1921), 34–37.

Abraham, a Jew, at the instance of Jehannot de Chevigny, goes to the court of Rome, and having marked the evil life of the clergy, returns to Paris, and becomes a Christian.

... In Paris, gracious ladies, as I have heard tell, there was once a great merchant, a large dealer in drapery, a good man, most loyal and righteous, his name Jehannot de Chevigny, between whom and a Jew, Abraham by name, also a merchant, and a man of great wealth, as also most loyal and righteous, there subsisted a very close friendship. Now Jehannot, observing Abraham's loyalty and rectitude, began to be sorely vexed in spirit that the soul of one so worthy and wise and good should perish for want of faith. Wherefore he began in a friendly manner to plead with him, that he should leave the errors of the Jewish faith and turn to the Christian verity, which, being sound and holy, he might see daily prospering and gaining ground, whereas, on the contrary, his own religion was dwindling and was almost come to nothing. The Jew replied that he believed that there was no faith sound and holy except the Jewish faith, in which he was born, and in which he meant to live and die; nor would anything ever turn him from there. Nothing daunted, however, Jehannot some days afterwards began again to ply Abraham with similar arguments, explaining to him in such crude fashion as merchants use the reasons why our faith is better than the Jewish. And though the Jew was a great master in the Jewish law, yet, whether it was by reason of his friendship for Jehannot, or that the Holy Spirit dictated the words that the simple merchant used, at any rate the Jew began to be much interested in Jehannot's arguments, though still too staunch in his faith to suffer himself to be converted. But Jehannot was no less assiduous in plying him with argument than he was obstinate in adhering to his law, insomuch that at length the Jew, overcome by such incessant appeals, said:

"Well, well, Jehannot, thou wouldst have me become a Christian, and I am disposed to do so, provided I first go to Rome and there see him whom thou callest God's vicar on earth, and observe what manner of life he leads and his brother cardinals with him; and if such it be that thereby, in conjunction with thy words, I may understand that thy faith is better than mine, as thou hast sought to shew me, I will do as I have said: otherwise, I will remain as I am a Jew."

When Jehannot heard this, he was greatly distressed, saying to himself:

"I thought to have converted him; but now I see that the pains which I took for so excellent a purpose are all in vain; for, if he goes to the court of Rome and sees the iniquitous and foul life which the clergy lead there, so far from turning Christian, had he been converted already, he would without doubt relapse into Judaism."

Then turning to Abraham he said:

"Nay, but, my friend, why wouldst thou be at all this labor and great expense of travelling from here to Rome? to say nothing of the risks both by sea and by land which a rich man like thee must needs run. Thinkest thou not to find here one that can give thee baptism? And as for any doubts that thou mayst have touching the faith to which I point thee, where wilt thou find greater masters and sages therein than here, to resolve thee of any question thou mayst put to them? Wherefore in my opinion this journey of thine is superfluous. Think that the prelates there are such as thou mayst have seen here, nay, as much better as they are nearer to the Chief Pastor. And so, by my advice thou wilt spare thy pains until some time of indulgence, when I, perhaps, may be able to bear thee company."

The Jew replied:

"Jehannot, I doubt not that so it is as thou sayst; but once and for all I tell thee that I am minded to go there, and will never otherwise do that which thou wouldst have me and hast so earnestly besought me to do."

"Go then," said Jehannot, seeing that his mind was made up, "and good luck go with thee"; and so he gave up the contest because nothing would be lost, though he felt sure that he would never become a Christian after seeing the court of Rome. The Jew took horse, and posted with all possible speed to Rome; where on his arrival he was honorably received by his fellow Jews. He said nothing to any one of the purpose for which he had come; but began circumspectly to acquaint himself with the ways of the Pope and the cardinals and the other prelates and all the courtiers; and from what he saw for himself, being a man of great intelligence, or learned from others, he discovered that without distinction of rank they were all sunk in the most disgraceful lewdness, sinning not only in the way of nature but after the manner of the men of Sodom, without any restraint of remorse or shame, in such sort that, when any great favor was to be procured, the influence of the courtesans and boys was of no small moment. Moreover he found them one and all gluttonous, wine-bibbers, drunkards, and next after lewdness, most addicted to the shameless service of the belly, like brute beasts.

And, as he probed the matter still further, he perceived that they were all so greedy and avaricious that human, nay Christian blood, and things sacred of what kind soever, spiritualities no less than temporalities, they bought and sold for money; which traffic was greater and employed more brokers than the drapery trade and all the other trades of Paris put together; open simony and gluttonous excess being glossed under such specious terms as "arrangement" and "moderate use of creature comforts," as if God could not penetrate the thoughts of even the most corrupt hearts, to say nothing of the signification of words, and would suffer Himself to be misled after the manner of men by the names of things. Which matters, with many others which are not to be mentioned, our modest and sober-minded Jew found by no means to his liking, so that, his curiosity being fully satisfied, he was minded to return to Paris; which accordingly he did. There, on his arrival, he was met by Jehannot; and the two made great cheer together. Jehannot expected Abraham's conversion least of all things, and allowed him some days of rest before he asked what he thought of the Holy Father and the cardinals and the other courtiers. To which the Jew forthwith replied:

"I think God owes them all an evil recompense: I tell thee, so far as I was able to carry my investigations, holiness, devotion, good works or exemplary living in any kind was nowhere to be found in any clerk; but only lewdness, avarice, gluttony, and the like, and worse, if worse may be, appeared to be held in such honor of all, that (to my thinking) the place is a center of diabolical rather than of divine activities. To the best of my judgment, your Pastor, and by consequence all that are about him devote all their zeal and ingenuity and subtlety to devise how best and most speedily they may bring the Christian religion to nought and banish it from the world. And because I see that what they so zealously endeavor does not come to pass, but that on the contrary your religion continually grows, and shines more and more clear, therein I seem to discern a very evident token that it, rather than any other, as being more true and holy than any other, has the Holy Spirit for its foundation and support. For which cause, whereas I met your exhortations in a harsh and obdurate temper, and would not become a Christian, now I frankly tell you that I would on no account omit to become such. Go we then to the church, and there according to the traditional rite of your holy faith let me receive baptism."

Jehannot, who had anticipated a diametrically opposite conclusion, as soon as he heard him so speak, was the best pleased man that ever was in the world. So taking Abraham with him to Notre Dame he prayed the clergy there to baptize him. When they heard that it was his own wish, they forthwith did so, and Jehannot raised him from the sacred font, and named him Jean; and afterwards he caused teachers of great eminence thoroughly to instruct him in our faith, which he readily learned, and afterwards practiced in a good, a virtuous, nay, a holy life.

2

The Life of Cola di Rienzo
ca. 1358

*In the mid-fourteenth century, Cola di Rienzo led and was a key opening
player in the effort by Renaissance Romans to establish a secular civic
government, such as the city had enjoyed in antiquity. In his own time the
effort failed. It was achieved only with the unification of Italy in the nineteenth century, a tardy but essential legacy of the Renaissance's crucial
contest between church and state in Rome as throughout Christendom.
This document provides a rich narrative of Cola di Rienzo's triumphal
moment as well as a harrowing description of the public desecration of
his corpse. The account of Cola's death offers a vivid reminder that the
Roman people's taste for blood, spectacle, and vengeance was not limited
to the ancients in the Colosseum but continued well into the Renaissance
and was a feature of life in the city. To what degree the crowd's anger
reflected popular outrage over Cola's policies or, instead, constituted
manipulation by the Colonna family for personal vengeance remains an
open question. The document is drawn from a larger, now fragmented
and partially lost chronicle of early fourteenth-century Roman history by
an unknown author.*

In those days, after Martino [di Porto, a tyrannical aristocrat] was
hanged, there was a festival of St. John in June [24, 1347]; all Rome
came to St. John in the morning. The Tribune [Cola di Rienzo] wished
to go to the festival like the others. This was how he went: he rode, with
a great company of knights, mounted on a white war horse, dressed
in white vestments lined with silk and decorated with gold laces. He
looked beautiful and terrifying at the same time; the hundred sworn
infantrymen of the region of Regola marched before him as he rode. A
banner was carried above his head.

On another day, after dinner, he rode to St. Peter's of Rome; men and
women ran to see him. This was the order of his beautiful procession:
first came a militia of armed horsemen, handsomely adorned, who later

John Wright, trans., *The Life of Cola di Rienzo* (Toronto: Pontifical Institute of Mediaeval
Studies, 1975), 51–53, 134–35, 146–48, 151–53.

were to march against the Prefect. They were followed by the officials, judges, notaries, chamberlains, chancellors, Senate scribes, and all the officials, Peacemakers, and syndics. Then followed four marshals with their customary mounted escort, and then, following these, Janni de Allo, who carried a goblet of gilded silver in his hand with the offering that the Tribune was to make, as is done for a Senator. After him came the horse soldiers and after them the trumpeters playing silver trumpets. The crashing silver cymbals made a noble and magnificent sound. Then came the town criers; all these people passed by in silence. After these came a single man who carried in his hand a naked sword, as a sign of justice; he was Buccio, son of Jubileo. After him followed a man who went through all the streets throwing and scattering money, as is done in the Emperor's processions. Liello Migliaro was his name; on either side of him there were two men who carried sacks of money. After these the Tribune followed alone. He rode a great war horse, and was dressed in fur-lined silk, half green and half yellow. In his right hand he carried a brightly polished steel rod; on its summit was an apple of gilded silver, and above the apple a little cross of gold, which contained wood from the True Cross; and on one side letters were enameled which read DEUS, and on the other SPIRITUS SANCTUS. Directly after him came Cecco d'Alesso, who carried a standard above his head, as is done for a king. The field of this standard was white, with a sun of shining gold in the middle, surrounded by silver stars. On top of the standard was a white dove of silver which carried an olive crown in its beak. On his right and left marched fifty vassals of Vitorchiano, the True Men with pikes in hand; they looked very much like bears, dressed and armed. After them followed the company of civilians: rich men, aristocrats, councilors, allies, and many other notable people. With such a triumph, with such glory he crossed the bridge of St. Peter, while everyone waved. The gates and barricades had been demolished; the streets were clear and free. After he arrived at the steps of St. Peter's, the Canons and all the clergy came out to meet him, solemnly dressed and prepared with white surplices, with the cross and incense; they came as far as the stairs singing VENI CREATOR SPIRITUS and received him with great rejoicing. Kneeling before the altar he made his offering; the clergy entrusted the possessions of St. Peter's to his care. . . .

[After several years in exile, Cola triumphantly returns to Rome.]

[H]is arrival became known in Rome. The Romans joyfully prepared to welcome him; the aristocrats were on the alert, watching closely. He left Orte and went to Rome, in the year of our Lord thirteen fifty-three. The cavalry of Rome came all the way out to Monte Mario to meet him, with branches of olive in their hands as a sign of victory and peace. The people welcomed him joyfully, as if he were Scipio Africanus. Triumphal arches were built. He entered the Castel Sant' Angelo gate. Throughout the piazza of the Castel Sant' Angelo and the bridge, and the streets, arches made of bunting were hung, and ornaments of gold and silver. It seemed that all Rome could scarcely contain itself for joy. The happiness and good will of the people could not have been greater.

So he was honorably escorted up to the Palace of the Campidoglio, where he delivered a beautiful and eloquent speech. He said that for seven years he had been exiled from his home, as Nebuchadnezzar had been [either Cola di Rienzo in his speech or the author of this document inverted the biblical exile story], but now, through the power of the virtuous God, he had returned to his senatorial seat by the voice of the Pope: not because he was worthy of such an office, but the Pope's voice had made him worthy. He added that he intended to raise up and reform the government of Rome. Then he made Messer Bettrone and Messer Arimbaldo de Narba Captains of War and gave them the banner of Rome; he made a certain Cecco de Peroscia, his councillor, a knight, and dressed him in gold.

The Romans held a great festival for him, as the Jews did for Christ, when He entered Jerusalem mounted on an ass. They honored Him, spreading carpets and olive branches before Him, singing: BENE-DICTUS QUI VENIS. Finally they went home and left Him alone with His disciples in the piazza; there was no one who offered Him a little dinner. . . .

[Cola di Rienzo's death.]

Now I want to describe the death of the Tribune. The Tribune had levied a tax on wine and other commodities, which he called a "subsidy." It amounted to six pennies per load of wine. He collected a great deal of money. The Romans put up with it in order to have a government. To increase his revenues he also rationed salt, and lowered his personal and household expenses. His only thoughts were for his soldiers. Without warning he arrested a noble and worthy citizen of Rome, named Panalfuccio de Guido. He was a noble man, who wanted to be lord of the people; Cola cut off his head without pity or cause. At his death all Rome was disturbed.

The Romans were like quiet little sheep; they dared not speak; they feared the Tribune like a demon. When the council met he got everything he wanted; no councilor contradicted him. He would laugh and weep at the same instant, and pouring out tears and sighs he would laugh, so volatile and mobile was his will. Now he wept, now he caroused.

Then he began arresting people; he arrested one man after another, and released them for ransom. The murmuring sounded quietly through Rome. Therefore to protect himself he enlisted fifty Roman infantrymen for each region of the city, ready at every alarm. He did not give them pay. He promised it. Every day he kept them in hire; he promised them a great deal of grain and other rewards. Finally, he dismissed Liccardo from his office and appointed new captains. This was his downfall. Liccardo ceased his looting and other military operations, grumbling, not unjustly, about Cola's ingratitude.

It was the month of September, the eighth day. Cola di Rienzi was in bed that morning. He had washed his face. Suddenly from the northeast there came a voice crying, "Long live the people! Long live the people!" At this voice the people came through the streets from this side and that. The cry grew louder; more people gathered. At the market crossroads armed men gathered; they came from Sant' Angelo and from Ripa; they came from Colonna and from Trevi. When they had assembled, the cry was changed, and they said, "Death to the traitor Cola di Rienzi! Death!"

Now the young men crowded around in a rage, the very ones who were enlisted in the Tribune's militia. All of the regions of the city were not there, only those which have been named. They ran to the Palace of the Campidoglio. Then other people joined them, men and women and children. They threw rocks; they made noise and uproar; they surrounded the Palace on every side, in front and behind, saying, "Death to the traitor who made the tax! Death!" Their rage was terrible. . . .

Cecco dello Viecchio took a dagger in his hand and stabbed him in the stomach.

He was the first. Immediately afterward Laurentio de Treio, the notary, struck his head with a sword. Then one man after another stabbed him; one struck, another swore to. He made no sound; he died at once; he felt no pain. A man came with a rope and tied his feet together. They threw him on the ground, dragging him and peeling off his skin; they pierced him until he looked like a sieve. Everyone joked about it; they seemed to be at a festival. In this way he was dragged as far as San Marcello. There he was hung from a balcony by the feet: he had no head. The bones of his skull were left behind on the road where he had been dragged. He had so many wounds that he looked like a sieve. There was no place without a wound. His fat guts dangled from his belly. He was horribly fat. He was white as bloody milk. He was so fat that he looked like a giant buffalo or cow in a slaughterhouse. He hung there two days and one night. The boys threw rocks at him. On the third day, at the command of Jugurta and Sciarretta della Colonna, he was dragged to the Campo dell'Austa.

There all the Jews were gathered, a great multitude; not one was left behind. There a fire of dry thistles was made; he was put in this fire of thistles. He was fat; because he was so fat he burnt easily and freely. The Jews were very busy there, hurrying, crowded; they stirred the thistles to make them burn. Thus the corpse was burnt and reduced to powder; not a speck was left. Such was the end of Cola di Rienzi, who made himself Tribune August of Rome, who wanted to be champion of the Romans.

3

CATHERINE OF SIENA

Letter to Pope Gregory XI

ca. September 13, 1376

Catherine of Siena (1347–1380) is the co-patron saint (with Francis of Assisi and Bernardine of Siena) of all of Italy and without doubt the most influential female saint in the history of the Dominican order. Holy women consciously emulated her spirituality for centuries after her death at age thirty-three by self-imposed fasting and dehydration, although she warned that her ways were not for everyone. She may have been illiterate, as were most fourteenth-century women of low status, or it may be true that she miraculously acquired the skills of reading and writing. Altogether, there are 381 letters written or dictated by her to family members, popes, kings and queens, soldiers of fortune, aristocrats, artists, disciples, monks and nuns, priests, and humble artisans. Likely due to her charisma, everyone, from the highest prelates to her scolding mother, heeded her words as if they were commands transmitted directly by God.

In the excerpted letter below, she urges the French-born Pope Gregory XI to overcome his fear of being poisoned should he return the papacy

D. Umberto Meattini, ed., *Santa Caterina da Siena: Epistolario* (Rome: Paoline, 1966), 109–15.

to Rome. It is his duty, she writes, to end what she considers to be the exile of the papacy in Avignon. She has traveled all the way from Siena to this French city with a formidable entourage of followers, including her confessor, and shortly she will relocate to Rome to continue giving advice to popes on how to reform the church. Gregory XI's fears for his life were not unfounded; he died within a year of his return, although not from poisoning. Saint Catherine's efforts at moral reform of the papacy did not succeed, but this failure in no way diminishes the importance of her voice, so distinctly female, in defending the centrality of Rome to all of Christendom, despite the city's bad reputation.

In the name of Jesus Christ crucified and of sweet Mary.

Most holy and most reverend sweet father in Christ sweet Jesus, your poor unworthy and miserable daughter Caterina, servant and slave of the servants of Jesus Christ, writes to your Holiness in his precious blood with the desire of seeing you strong and persevering in your good and holy resolve, and in such a way that no contrary wind can impede you, neither a devil nor anyone else. It seems that they want to come, as our Savior says in his Holy Gospel, in sheep's clothing looking like lambs, [but] they are rapacious wolves. . . .

It seems to me, therefore, this venomous man on one side commends your return [to Rome], saying it is good and holy, but on the other side he says that poison is being prepared. And it seems to me he counsels you to send some trusted men to go ahead of you, to find the poison that is put on the tables, and more specifically in the bottles, which is prepared for slow administration, over days, or months or a year. Well, I must confess that poison may be found just as well on the tables of Avignon as in other cities, just like at those of Rome. . . .

And it seems to me he wants to do with you as the child's mother does to him when she wants to take away the milk from his mouth. She puts something bitter on her breast so that he tastes the bitterness before the milk, so that for fear of the bitter he abandons the sweet; because a child is deceived more by bitterness than by anything else. That is what he wants to do to you, first setting forth the bitterness of poison and much persecution to trick the innocence of your tender sensitive love, so that out of fear you give up the milk; the very milk of Grace that will follow your sweet return. And I pray you on behalf of Christ crucified not to be a timid child but manly. Open your mouth and swallow the bitter for the sweet. It does not become your Holiness to abandon milk because of the bitterness. I hope for, in the infinite and inestimable goodness of God that, if you are willing, he will bestow upon you and us [his] grace; and I hope that you will be firm and steady, not to be moved by any sort of wind or demonic illusion, nor by advice from a devil incarnate; instead you will follow the will of God and your good desire, and the advice of the servants of Jesus Christ crucified.

I say no more. . . . Forgive me, father, for such overly presumptuous talk. Humbly I ask you to pardon me and to give me your blessing. Remain in the holy and sweet delight of God. I pray that his infinite goodness will give me the grace soon, for his honor, of seeing you put your foot across the doorway, with peace, rest and quiet in soul and body. I beg you, sweet father, that when it pleases your Holiness, you grant me an audience because I would like to find myself in front of you before I leave. The time is short, so, if it pleases you, I would like to meet as soon as possible. Sweet Jesus, Jesus love!

2

Renaissance Romans

4

GIOVANNI MATTIOTTI

Francesca Romana

ca. 1440

Francesca Bussa de' Ponziani (1384–1440), universally known as Francesca Romana, is the co-patron saint of Rome (with Philip Neri). She was born in the well-to-do Parione district (see Map, p. xviii, District VI) to an old Roman family of the lesser nobility and betrothed at age twelve to a papal military officer, Rienzo de' Ponziani. Only after a year's delay, during which she suffered a paralytic illness, was her marriage consummated, and in the next five years she gave birth to three children. For the rest of her days she was a dutiful wife and mother while also engaged in prodigious charitable work on the streets of Rome. Assisted by her sister-in-law, Vannozza, she tended to the homeless camped near the Tiber River, tirelessly carrying a lantern through the night as she encouraged men and women down on their luck to take shelter at one of Rome's hospices.

Giovanni Mattiotti, Francesca Romana's parish priest, wrote the document excerpted below. He is the earliest and most reliable witness to the events of her life, having heard her frequent confessions and served as her spiritual adviser during her last ten years. Although secrets are protected in the Catholic confessional, the confessor of a saint-to-be is allowed to tell the world of his penitent's virtues. The excerpt relates several troubling aspects of Francesca Romana's adolescence and her married life. Her

Giorgio Carpaneto, *Il dialetto romanesco del quattrocento: Il manoscritto quattrocentesco di G. Mattiotti narrai i tempi, i personaggi, le "visioni" di Santa Francesca Romana, compatrona di Roma* ([S.I.], NES, 1995), 1, 2, 4, 6, 17, 31.

confessor and her devotees saw these events as testimony to her holiness. The incidents and feelings described may also be used cautiously as evidence about the possible experiences of other early Renaissance Roman women.

I, Father Giovanni, unworthy spiritual father of the devout servant of the Most High God, blessed Francesca, make manifest some things which came to my knowledge about her life and the graces granted to her by God the Highest. This blessed Francesca was the daughter of the noble Roman citizen named Paolo Bussa and of the noble Roman woman named Madame [Iacovella Rofredeschi]. This blessed Francesca, from her infancy was totally pure and so bashful before worldly things that not only did she not converse but she was not seen by any man, so much so that she could not stand the touch of her own father. And when she was espoused at the age of twelve to her husband, named Rienzo Ponziani, a noble Roman citizen, she was immediately struck with a serious illness, which lasted a long time. Upon being pushed by her family to seek medical care, she refused to consent to such divine offence. And upon being cured of this infirmity, after a short while she was visited with an even greater malady, one that lasted for the space of a year, during which time she was entirely lost and could not even assist herself. Then there came a woman who exhorted the blessed to let a witch cure her of her illness; [Francesca], having great abomination for such a thing and zealous for truth, threw her out. And the following night the glorious Saint Alessio [a popular local Roman saint] came to her in a vision on his feast day in the form of a beautiful youth, and he said these words twice: "Do you want to be healthy?" And the blessed answered that she wished whatever God willed, and immediately she was healed and liberated. Arising the next morning, she called her beloved sister-in-law Vannozza and the worthy Vannozza, having always assisted her in her grave illness, said: "Is that you Ceccolella [little Francesca]?" And then, rejoicing, together with the men of the household, they went to the church of Saint Alessio. This turn of events was greatly admired by all the people who knew of Francesca's grave illness, seeing her now perfectly healthy. . . .

[Father Giovanni's account continues below with an event on a later occasion, one meant to reflect on Francesca's virtues but that also reveals much about daily life in Rome.]

Returning one day from the church of Saint Peter, the blessed and her sister-in-law, feeling especially hot and thirsty, and being at the church of Saint Leonard, went down to the Tevere [Tiber River] to get a drink, whereupon both of them fell into the river; submerged in the water and nearly drowning, for the great love they had for each other they held hands. Because of the intimate affection this servant of God had for Vannozza, she feared for her death more than her own, and Vannozza for the blessed servant of Christ's death. They did not realize where the river carried them until they found themselves wet but on the shore. . . .

[The narrative later tells of Francesca's eating habits, describing her virtues and by implication the habits of other Romans.]

The blessed servant of Christ was so temperate that whether in summer or winter she ate only one meal per day except that in the summer because of the long days she would take a piece of fruit or a leaf of lettuce. As she told me, her unworthy spiritual father, she ate no fish, neither fresh nor salted, and only rarely a little fresh meat. This blessed never drank wine but only pure water. She did not eat chickens nor eggs, whether she was healthy or sick. No sugar and no apples or food made from them. No syrups or medicines. Her food consisted of herbs, legumes conditioned only with salt and no oil; she ate fruits in season, beans, and similar things of little substance. These things she ate with no pleasure because she had lost her sense of taste. . . .

[Father Mattioli relates intimate details of her sexual life as a married woman.]

So great was her gentility that when her husband called for the marital debt [the obligation of married persons to respond to requests for sex] she suffered distress beyond belief, so much that her stomach became upset and stopped up so terribly that once she spit up blood. So much so that her husband, moved by compassion, no longer demanded the marital debt, and this happened before I was her spiritual director, because the entire time that I, Father Giovanni, confessed the servant of Christ, she did not have sex but lived in holy chastity. . . .

[Francesca Romana experienced frightening dreams, some of which included demonic tours of Rome.]

While the blessed servant of Christ lived in her husband's house, one night while she was in holy meditation, twenty-six demons came to molest her, as always happened when she engaged in her spiritual exercises. They were very fearsome and horrible, very ferocious and enflamed, holding torches and harshly insulting her, saying: "This is justice and the wrath of God that he sends on the city of Rome for the great iniquities that take place here. And two of them wanted to go through each district of Rome, to do great damage. Whereupon this blessed, being greatly in awe both for the great molestation these horrible visions caused in her and for the evil to befall Rome, took refuge in divine consolation. . . . [The narrative relates that God banished the demons but warned Francesca that] if the Romans do not repent, great ruin will come to them. And then lightning struck. The first bolt [fell] on the bell tower of Saint Paul, the second on the bell tower of Saint Peter and the other on the chapel of the Lord of Saint John. And this happened in the year of our Lord 1430 in the month of July. Glory to the Lord. . . .

[Another vision recounts elements of hostility toward Jews, in this instance related to Jewish domination of the used clothing market in Rome.]

Another time, [she saw] Christ stripped and flagellated at the column. Then, desiring to get dressed, Christ could not find his clothes because the Jews had hidden them. As he searched for his garments the Jews' dogs followed him and bit at him ferociously.

5

JOHANNES BURCHARDUS

Lucretia Borgia and Her Family

1501

In the history of Renaissance Rome, the reputation of Pope Alexander VI (Roderic Llançol i Borja, or Rodrigo Borgia; r. 1492–1503) and his family for wanton behavior is second to none. During her lifetime and ever since, Rodrigo's illegitimate daughter, Lucretia (or Lucrezia), has been a target of outrage and salacious gossip. Wild rumors and charges circulated in her own day: incest with her brother Cesare and/or with her father Rodrigo, birth of an illegitimate child at the time that her first marriage was annulled for non-consummation, drowning of two of her servants to prevent them from testifying against her, and poisoning of other enemies, along with better documented extramarital affairs throughout her third and most stable marriage with Alfonso d'Este, Duke of Ferrara. It is little wonder that Lucretia has been the favored female subject of the entire Italian Renaissance, appearing over the centuries in

F. L. Glaser, ed., *Pope Alexander VI and His Court: Extracts from the Latin Diary of Johannes Burchardus, Bishop of Orta and Civita Castellana, Pontifical Master of Ceremonies* (New York: Nicholas L. Brown, 1921), 152–55.

numerous novels, plays, operas, television series, and video games, all harshly critical of her alleged behavior. A more balanced view would add that she was a gifted intellectual and the only person her father trusted to handle papal matters while he was out of town or otherwise occupied. As the duchess of Ferrara beginning in 1502 and until her death during childbirth in 1519, she presided successfully over one of the Renaissance's most illustrious courts. In these years she thrived as a forceful independent woman, not the tool of her dead father or brother.

The document below is an eyewitness account recorded in the contemporary diary entries of Johannes Burchardus, master of ceremonies for Pope Alexander VI. It shares the outrage many Romans felt about the debauchery of the Borgia papal court. Especially noteworthy are the September 9 entry about a nameless murderess, likely from the lower ranks, and the routine tone with which Burchardus reports that while the pope was away for four weeks between September 25 and October 23, the thrice-married Lucretia was in charge of his quarters.

On Saturday, the 4th of September, 1501, about vespers the news came from Ferrara of the conclusion of the marriage contract between Alfonso, the first-born of the Duke of Ferrara and Lucretia Borgia. Therefore bombards were set off continuously from the castle of San Angelo from then until into the night. On the following Sunday after breakfast Lucretia rode from the palace where she resided to the church Santa Maria del Popolo, dressed in a robe of golden brocade accompanied by about three hundred on horseback. Before her rode four bishops, namely Hieronymus de Porcarris, Vincenz Pistachio, Petrus Gamba, and Antonio Flores, two by two. Then followed Lucretia alone and, after her, her suite and servants. In the same way she returned to the palace.

On the same day the main bell of the Capitol was rung from the hour of supper until the third hour in the night. Numerous fires were lighted in the castle of San Angelo and over the whole city. The towers of the castle and the Capitol and others were illuminated in order to excite everybody to joy, though shame would have been more fitting.

On the following Monday two jugglers, to one of whom on horseback Donna Lucretia had given her new robe of brocade worn only once on the previous day and worth three hundred ducats, went through all the main streets and alleys of Rome with the loud cry: "Long live the noble Duchess of Ferrara, long live Pope Alexander! Long may they live." And then the other one on foot to whom Donna Lucretia had also given a robe went along with the same cry.

On Thursday, the 9th of September, 1501, there was hung at the wall of the Torre di Nona a woman who had stabbed her husband to death with a knife during the previous night.

On Saturday, the 25th of September, the Pope went early in the morning to Nepi, Civita Castellana, and to the other places in the neighborhood, and with him Cesare Borgia and the Cardinals Serra, Francesco and Ludovico Borgia, with a small suite. Donna Lucretia remained in the chamber of the Pope in order to guard it and with the same orders as upon the previous absence of the Pope. He returned to Rome on Saturday, the 23rd of October, 1501.

On the evening of the last day of October, 1501, Cesare Borgia arranged a banquet in his chambers in the Vatican with fifty honest prostitutes, called courtesans, who danced after the dinner with the attendants and others who were present, at first in their garments, then naked. After the dinner the candelabra with the burning candles were taken from the tables and placed on the floor, and chestnuts were strewn around, which the naked courtesans picked up, creeping on hands and knees between the chandeliers, while the Pope, Cesare, and his sister Lucretia looked on. Finally prizes were announced for those who could perform the act most often with the courtesans, such as tunics of silk, shoes, barrets, and other things.

On Monday, the 11th of November, 1501, there entered the city through the Porta Viridarii a peasant leading two mares laden with wood. When these arrived in the place of St. Peter the men of the Pope ran towards them and cut the saddle-bands and ropes, and throwing down the wood they led the mares to the small place that is inside the palace just behind the portal. There four stallions freed from reins and bridles were sent from the palace and they ran after the mares and with a great struggle and noise fighting with tooth and hoof jumped upon the mares and covered them, tearing and hurting them severely. The Pope stood together with Donna Lucretia under the window of the chamber above the portal of the palace and both looked down at what was going on there with loud laughter and much pleasure.

6

Song of the Penitential Lay-Sisters Gone to Rome

Fifteenth or Sixteenth Century

*Carnival songs (*canti carnascialeschi*) originated in Florence and spread throughout the Italian peninsula. They are a wonderful source of information about popular culture as it emerged during festival days, such as those celebrated just before Lent. The authorship of the songs, the existence of variations, and whether some of the songs were ever sung are unknown.*

The song reprinted below makes fun of pinzochere, *translated here with the formal term "penitential lay-sisters." Within church regulations, pinzochere were tertiaries, or third-order religious, distinguishing them from monks (first-order) and nuns (second-order). Unlike nuns, many of them had been denied formal vows and entry into a convent because they were married, because they were judged to have led sinful past lives, or because they lacked the dowry and other requirements for formal admission to a recognized order. Others freely chose the status of tertiary so that they might live in the world while following strict penitential practices and engaging in good works. Romans knew and venerated holy tertiaries such as Catherine of Siena (Document 3) and their own Francesca Romana (Document 4). But Rome's streets also abounded with not-quite-reformed prostitutes, women forced by a local magistrate or induced by a zealous priest to abandon the sex trade and now engaged in selling magic potions to enhance beauty or sexual desire. Such women were popularly ridiculed as* pinzochere *and are the subjects of the song that follows.*

Song of the Penitential Lay-Sisters Gone to Rome

Women, we once were as you now are,
Courtesans and famous for beauty:
Now, close to old age,
Penitent lay-sisters we are, as you see.

Charles S. Singleton, ed., *Canti Carnascialeschi* (Bari, It.: Laterza, 1936), 121–23.

We seem to be removed from mundane pleasures,
From what appears on the outside:
But the secret is not so inside yet,
Since our thoughts
Are the same still;
But under the shadow of a quieter living,
Going back and forth,
We provide support to those whom love troubles
Always serving heartily and with faith.

And to show you what we can do,
In these little boxes
We have brought all our art:
Like hand by hand
Will be shown to you
The things that are good side by side:
Firstly, these are cards
Not born by spells or enchantments,
As we can do through various means.

Quick shake of women and noctules
Heads of hanged men,
Bones of dead and fat men we have,
Pennies taken to the cross,
And consecrated papal letters
That we obtained with great difficulty
Nails and hairs,
Holy pictures and blessed candles,
With which we make the people go by force.

Many other things we would have to show you
That are good at this art,
With which we do stupendous things:
But we would be tedious.
Passing to the other wise
Where our virtue spreads greatly,
Among which are comprised
Many beautiful things that we want
To show you, beautiful women, and they will be dear to you.

Distilled waters of different kinds,
To make the skin whiter

Stretch the wrinkle and harden the breast:
If one is strong,
They can always be used
For everything, below and above, with delight.
For who has the defect
Of moaning or sweating somewhere else,
We have tested marvelous remedies.

Then glasses and pliers to pluck eyelashes,
And dust of teeth,
With leeches, sponges, perfumes and patches
Full of wonder
With sublimate of mercury unguents
That where you put them, hair never grows again;
And to remove neat
Spots, cloth and haze from the face,
Remedies really made in heaven.

We still have many other beautiful secrets
To make abortions
And to return the virginal cloth
With which for many priests
We have allowed the taste
Many times of a woman as virgin, who
Lost her mind
A short while before giving birth, for love
Of saving her honor, with our help.

Yet, discrete and lovely women,
Foresee the evil
That old age brings with itself:
If you want to learn from us
All these things,
We'll teach you out of kindness;
Since, once beauty fades,
We remind you that it is better to be a porter
Than to be a miserable washerwoman or a foot soldier.

7

Pasquinades

Sixteenth Century

*Pasquinades—anonymous short poems of political satire—derive their
name from the fact that at least some of them (all, by tradition, but that
is unlikely) were originally placed during the night upon the statue of
Pasquino, located at the edge of Piazza Navona, a central gathering
place for Rome's people. Here poetic Romans could vent their spleens
and poke fun at their fellow citizens, everyone from the pope to the city's
most noble ladies. Posting these little ditties ostensibly served as a safety
valve by allowing the expression of negative opinion against ruling elites,
although the political import of this form of protest surely was minimal.
Only the humorless Pope Clement VII had the temerity to ban the practice, an order that denied Romans one of their favorite literary sports and
produced no offsetting gains for his prestige or popularity.*

*The named target of the first two selections, Vittoria Farnese (1521–
1602), successfully resisted her father's initial nuptial plans for her. The
duke of Savoy mentioned in the poem presumably is Charles III, Duke of
Savoy, who had been widowed in 1538 when he was fifty-two and Vittoria
only seventeen. Eventually, at the mature age of twenty-seven, she married a man more to her liking, the widower Guidobaldo II della Rovere,
Duke of Urbino. A poetic attack on her, everyone understood, was also
an attack on her grandfather, none other than Pope Paul III (Alessandro
Farnese), who held the papacy from 1534 to 1549, as well as on her
illustrious parents, the pope's illegitimate son and career mercenary, Pier
Luigi, and the noble Gerolama Orsini. Madame Orsini was well-known
by her contemporaries for her extraordinarily tolerant comportment in
the face of her husband's openly dissolute lifestyle, which included public
sexual encounters and exploitative debauchery with people of both sexes.*

*The third selection satirizes Rome's proper matrons for their willing-
ness to accept the rule of men, both civic senators and high clerics, who*

Valerio Marucci, Antonio Marzo, and Angelo Romano, eds., *Pasquinate Romane del
Cinqueccento* (Rome: Salerno Editrice, 1983), vol. 1, 519–22, 694–95.

*elevated the status of courtesans at the expense of good Christian women.
The poem closes with another swipe at the pope for not being a servant of
his people. Taken together, these pasquinades shed light on the way everyday Romans were ready to poke fun at the human foibles they witnessed,
whether committed by women or men of high station or low.*

To Madame Vittoria Farnese—Sonnet 482

Vittoria, since the world doesn't want you
And no partner for you is to be found,
Don't wait anymore for your [parents] to find you a husband:
They feed you with wind and words.

Now that you are beautiful, as beautiful as the sun,
Find a lover pleasing and favored,
And with him satiate that sweet appetite,
That so often molests you.

Your clear and beautiful serenity flees with the years,
The beauty, the joy of your sweet face,
And the supreme good that Love has put in your bosom.

If you want to wait until the duke of Savoy [Charles III, the Good]
Comes to marry you, or that of Lorraine [probably Francis I],
You'll become old first and you'll die of lust.

Pasquinade on Madame Vittoria Farnese—Sonnet 483

The beauty Vittoria Farnese cries and suffers
And to the mother duchess complains,
And whines also with the father,
That they are giving her such a discourteous husband.

My dear father, she says, from you came
These plots, to me so obscure and dark,
To content your dishonest desires
And to be an outrage against me, who ever offended you?

Why now you have the whim to consent
With the holy father to such a strange appetite,
Of giving me to that deformed man of Savoy [Charles II, the Good]?

My life will always be in the cruel boredom
Of having such a monster as my husband,
That just thinking of it, only death suits me.

But before I should ever
Consent to this arrangement, I want first that
My life be destroyed by you.

Alas, bitter and wicked fortune,
Couldn't I die when I fell,
So that I would not be now in so many tribulations and fixes?

Miserable me, I hoped,
Seeing a pope and a duke in high position,
I didn't have to be considered as garbage.

All that was missing was to marry
That church man of Anconese country [possibly Benedetto Accolti],
Or at least he could give me to the Colonna [Fabrizio Colonna]!

Oh sad desires ignited,
To please the thieving imperator,
The evil shepherd wants this for me.

And how great is the pain,
I cannot yet say, that Vittoria
I don't want to call myself anymore, but end of glory.

And leaving that memory
Of myself before I die, and such a manifest one,
Be eternal infamy on the house of Farnese.

Pasquinade to the Women of Rome—Sonnet 600

Oh graceful women and Roman souls of mine,
It grieves me that your great senate
Has given your name little by little
Even to the harlots,

Tolerating that even the bootlickers
Go around clothed in your white dress,
And that their condition cannot be distinguished from yours,
Impious, ribald, and honor's desecrator!

If you do not deal with this, my women,
It would be better for you to change your dress
And lose your old habit.

Go to the councilor with great boldness,
And tell him to deal with this matter,
Otherwise, you will go tell it to the shepherd.

8

POPE PAUL IV

Since It Is Absurd

1555

---

*Even when Catholic Reformation leaders focused primarily on responding
to Protestantism, their anti-Semitic convictions remained strong, as this
papal bull (edict) indicates. The bull carried the full weight of law in all
the lands of the Papal States, including Rome. According to Kenneth Stow,
the scholar whose translation follows, the introductory passage is evidence
of renewed papal interest in converting Jews. Not all historians agree
with Stow.[1]*

*There is less room for debate about the meaning of the numbered restric-
tions that follow the introduction. Clause 1 of the bull legally established
confinement of Jews to a ghetto, which was already largely the reality
in Rome, as shown in the 1526–1527 census of households. Clause 2
addressed the multiplicity of ethnically based synagogues mentioned in
Document 17, which was written two decades earlier. The remaining
clauses address a range of economic and social exchanges among Jews
and Christians. A good case could be made that the actions prohibited
by the bull must have been common in order to incur the pope's wrath.*

---

[1]David Berger, "*Cum Nimis Absurdum* and the Conversion of the Jews," *Jewish
Quarterly Review* 70, no. 1 (July 1979): 41–49.

Kenneth Stow, *Catholic Thought and Papal Jewry Policy, 1555–1593* (New York: Jewish
Theological Seminary of America, 1977), 294–98.

Overall, a picture emerges of Roman street life with Jews working and mingling side by side with Christians.

Since it is absurd and improper that Jews—whose own guilt has consigned them to perpetual servitude—under the pretext that Christian piety receives them and tolerates their presence should be ingrates to Christians, so that they attempt to exchange the servitude they owe to Christians for dominion over them; we—to whose notice it has lately come that these Jews, in our dear city and in some other cities, holdings, and territories of the Holy Roman Church, have erupted into insolence: they presume not only to dwell side by side with Christians and near their churches, with no distinct habit to separate them, but even to erect homes in the more noble sections and streets of the cities, holdings, and territories where they dwell, and to buy and possess fixed property, and to have nurses, housemaids, and other hired Christian servants, and to perpetrate many other things in ignominy and contempt of the Christian name—considering that the Roman Church tolerates the Jews in testimony of the true Christian faith and to the end [*ad hoc, ut*]* that they, led by the piety and kindness of the Apostolic See, should at length recognize their errors, and make all haste to arrive at the true light of the Catholic faith, and thereby [*propterea*] to agree that, as long as they persist in their errors, they should recognize through experience that they have been made slaves while Christians have been made free through Jesus Christ, God and our Lord, and that it is iniquitous that the children of the free woman should serve the children of the maid-servant—

1. Desiring to make sound provisions as best we can, with the help of God, in the above matter, we sanction by this our perpetually valid constitution that, among other things, in all future times in this city, as in all other cities, holdings, and territories belonging to the Roman Church, all Jews should live solely in one and the same location, or if that is not possible, in two or three or as many as are necessary, which are to be contiguous and separated completely from the dwellings of Christians. These places are to be designated by us in our city and by our magistrates in the other cities, holdings, and territories. And they should have one entry alone, and so too one exit.

---

*In this document only, all square bracket insertions are in the original translation, not additions by editor Rudolph Bell.

2. And in the individual cities, holdings, and territories where they dwell, they [the Jews] should have one synagogue alone in its customary location, and they may construct no new synagogue. Nor may they possess any real property. Accordingly, they must demolish and destroy all their [other] synagogues except for this one alone. The real property which they now possess, they must sell to Christians within a period of time designated by the local magistrates.

3. And so that they be identified everywhere as Jews, men and women are respectively required and bound to wear in full view a hat or some obvious marking, both to be blue in color, in such a way that they may not be concealed or hidden. Nor may they be excused from wearing the hat or marking on the pretext of rank, eminence, or privilege; nor may they acquire an absolution or dispensation through the ecclesiastical chamberlain, clerics of the Apostolic Camera or other persons presiding there, or through legates and vice-legates of the Apostolic See.

4. [And they shall not] have nurses or serving women or any other Christians serving them, of whatever sex. Nor shall they have their children wet-nursed or reared by Christian women.

5. Nor may they themselves or anyone in their employ labor in public on Sundays or other feast days declared by the Church.

6. Nor may they oppress Christians in any manner, [especially by] drawing up fictitious or simulated contracts [of debt].

7. Nor should they be so presumptuous as to entertain or dine with Christians or to develop close relations and friendships with them.

8. Nor may they use in the ledgers and account books which they have with Christians, [stipulating] the duration [of loans, etc.], any other alphabet than the Latin one or any other language than everyday Italian. If they do otherwise, these books will have no value [when brought as testimony in court] against Christians [who have defaulted on repayment].

9. Additionally, these Jews may carry on no business as purveyors of grain, barley, or other items necessary for human sustenance, but must be limited [in this sphere] to dealing only in second-hand clothing, the *arte cenciariae* (as it is commonly called).

10. As for those among them [the Jews] who are physicians, even if they are summoned and requested, they may not come forth and attend to the care of Christians.

11. Nor may they permit the Christian poor [or any other Christian for that matter] to address them as Master.

12. And in their computations and accounting, months must be composed of thirty fully completed days, and days that do not add up to the number thirty must be computed not as full months, but only as the actual number of days that have elapsed—and they [the Jews] may demand repayment only according to the number of days, not according to the rate for completed months. Pledges temporarily given them as collateral for their money, they may not sell for eighteen months, unless [otherwise] agreed upon prior to the day on which the pledges were actually given. After eighteen months have passed, if the Jews sell these pledges, all receipts over and above the value of the original loan must be made over to the owner of the pledge [i.e., the original borrower].

13. They will be held to observe without exception all statutes of the cities, holdings, and territories in which they dwell that give advantage to [lit. concern the favor of] Christians [over Jews].

14. And if they transgress the above in any way, either by us, or by our vicar, or by others deputized by us in the city, or by those same magistrates [noted above] in the other cities, holdings, and territories, they should be punished according to the nature of the transgression, either as rebels or perpetrators of the crime of *lèse majesté*, and as those who have renounced their allegiance to the entire Christian people, in accordance with the determination made by us or the vicars, deputies, and magistrates.

15. Notwithstanding the apostolic constitutions and ordinations and whatever apostolic tolerations, privileges, or indults[2] conceded to those Jews through any of our predecessors, the Roman pontiffs, or legates of that See, or chamberlains of this Roman Church, or clerics of the Apostolic Camera or others presiding there, under whatever decree or edict and with whatever limitations—even limitations of limitations—and other more valid and unusual clauses, and equally with other decrees and

[2]Papal licenses.

invalidations, indeed, by our own action and from our clear
knowledge and by the plenitude of apostolic power, and even by
approbations, and so too by changes which have been renewed
and approved repeatedly — with respect to all the foregoing, as
well as with respect to anything whatsoever contrary [to this
letter], even if in place of a general abrogation concerning
them and all their stipulations a special, specific, express, and
individual mention or whatever other expression has had to be
made or some carefully chosen form has had to be retained,
for each and every word and not only for the general clauses
themselves important, we, in this place, both specifically and
expressly, abrogate decrees of this kind, even if word for word,
with nothing at all omitted, and the traditional form preserved
in them they have been inserted [into this present letter], having expressed clearly in this letter that these decrees should
otherwise remain in force.

No one [may act against this letter], etc.
If anyone [so dares, he will call upon himself Apostolic censure], etc.
Given at Rome at St. Mark's, in the year of the Incarnation of the Lord
one thousand five hundred fifty-five, on the day before the Ides of July,
in the first year of our pontificate.

9

ALESSANDRO TRAJANO PETRONIO

On Roman Lifestyle and the Preservation of Good Health

1592

---

*The renowned medical doctor and philosopher Alessandro Petronio
(d. 1585) served as personal physician to Pope Gregory XIII (r. 1572–
1585), to whom his book is dedicated. He also counted his dear friend
Saint Ignatius of Loyola among the numerous patients he treated during
more than sixty years of medical practice in Rome. Petronio found time to
write several books, but only this one, translated from the original Latin
into Italian by Basilio Paravicino seven years after the doctor's death,
was aimed at a popular audience. It offers a rich portrait of the complexity of the city and its population. Especially noteworthy is Petronio's keen
and confident diagnostic assessment of the people's overall health and
how people, especially men, might have improved their health by following less indulgent lifestyles. Petronio's patients largely came from the elite
sector of society, but his observations in this excerpt extend to less fortunate Romans, including prostitutes and their offspring. The physician's
underlying physiological approach is based on humoral theory, which was
widely accepted during the Renaissance. It holds that men are naturally
hot and dry, whereas women tend to be cool and wet. Good health comes
with proper exercise and eating foods that maintain an appropriate balance of the four bodily humors.*

Chapter XXV. Who Are the People Who Live in Rome?

There are people of many varied nationalities in this City, but principally
Italians, Spanish, French and Germans: among these, some come and
go; others remain here more permanently: some stay for a little while,
some for a long time, others forever. Among these who remain in Rome,
only a few are very fat, many have an average build, and many are slim,

---

Alessandro Trajano Petronio, *Del viver delli Romani, et di conserver la Sanità* (Rome:
Domenico Basa, 1592), 196–204, 263–65.

but not yet worn-out. Among these there are many who have the habit of sitting like tailors and other similar workers, while a few exercise continuously. Some others (but these are very few) give themselves up to idleness, gluttony, and pleasures; the majority of them live with their souls in constant angst because they quarrel, or because they attend to their studies, or because they have given themselves up to seeking fame and fortune; or because, since they have put their whole aim in God, they direct all their thoughts to Him. Then there are the women, among whom very few are unmarried; the married ones are frequently pregnant. There are innumerable male and female infants, rarely nursed by their mothers, often put out to foreigner wet nurses. Among old people, one finds very few males and many more females, and this happens because males in their old age, and also during their youths and the rest of their lives, were very intemperate and lived in a disorderly way, whereas women lived decently during the whole time of their life. This is enough to be said about the people who live in Rome.

For what concerns nourishment, it is important to know that only a few fast; in fact they eat at least twice a day, and often more; and when it is not prohibited by the Church's commandments, they eat more meat than elsewhere, and this is because, since Rome's food is not very nutritious,[1] although abundant (as we said before), more often than not people are forced to eat quickly, and more often in large quantity and substance than in small amounts. In spring time, and especially during Lent they eat more vegetables and legumes, and in particular the poor eat a lot of cold cuts, and the rich eat abundantly of good fish and similar things. After Lent, during Easter time, the majority of people have a calcium-rich diet, especially *mozzarella di bufala*, butter, milk and other dairy products; for fifty days they consume great quantities of lamb and thereafter beef for the rest of the year. During summer there is always an abundance of vegetables, especially cabbages, and among these Savoy cabbages are the most prized, along with fruit of any sort, and melons.

Men frequently go to the vineyards with their whole family, where during the day they are baked by the sun; in the evening they dine out most of the time, and there, after working up a sweat, they often drink copiously and avidly strong wines chilled in the snow or in very cold caves. During fall and winter they eat chestnuts abundantly, and grapes as much as they can have; cabbages, and pork meat, and then

---

[1] Below, in explaining the high fertility of Roman women, the author contradicts himself about the nutritional quality of Rome's food.

they drink new Romanesco wine for flavoring. Then there are some religious people, who, since they are forbidden from eating meat, eat only cheese, eggs, and similar things. Those who are allowed to eat meat also regularly consume these foods. All these religious people fast often and, since they have to fast for long periods during the year such as during Lent, they also often fast from cheese, eggs, and from all the fatty foods, and they are content just with vegetables, legumes, and cold cuts, and other similar things, although sometimes, but rarely, they are given fish. I leave aside for the moment those who live so self-indulgently, and fill the body so copiously, never thinking about anything beyond satisfying daily their unbridled appetite, because there are only very few of them in this city. I have said the above about the food and drink habits.

Chapter XXVII. On Married Women, and Their Many Children

In this city married women are pregnant more often than elsewhere. As the land is fertile, and female wild animals have many offspring, so for the same reason women too are fertile. I am referring to those women who have intercourse only with their husbands, and not with infinite men, as prostitutes do instead. Prostitutes have coitus and move their genitals so often that their cervix hardens so much that it becomes almost a callus and it remains always open. Therefore, the spirit of the man's semen received into the cervix goes out of it immediately and vanishes. This is the very powerful cause of the fact that prostitutes do not have children. In case prostitutes have children, it is either because they do not have intercourses with men often, or because they neither toss nor are tormented too much during the coitus. But let's go back to our topic. As we said, married women are more fertile in this city because Rome is a humid and warm place most of the time, provided with every convenience, and an abundance of every nutritious food.

Moreover, this city is very similar to spring, when sown lands fructify better, and female animals get pregnant more easily, as the abundance and availability of food invite animals to eat, even when they are not hungry. Therefore, since semen is the superfluity of aliments, a great abundance of semen is generated; then, since they can easily have coitus, they easily get pregnant. This does not happen so often elsewhere, where either they do not have such an abundance of nutritious food or they live in greater distress than in Rome. This is the reason why there are so many male and female infants.

It is important to use great diligence in order to prevent the [infants] from getting the diseases to which they are very prone, especially if anyone arouses great fear in them—which they suffer enormously, since they are weak and therefore they are afraid of any little thing. Since their substance and flesh are so soft and tender, they also liquefy easily and they easily dissipate. This can readily be seen when one arouses fear in them, even a little bit, and immediately they uncontrollably poop or wet themselves, or both things at the same time; then joints-aches, or ear-aches, or aches of other body parts arise, and sometimes they have a fever that threatens their lives, as we have often observed.

10

GIOVANNI BELLORI

Michelangelo Merisi da Caravaggio: A Biography (1672) and an Inventory (1605)

Artists were both part of Rome's mainstream populations and influenced by them. The first selection below, from an early biographical account of the artist Michelangelo Merisi, known as Caravaggio (1571–1610), by Giovanni Bellori, tells us how this pathbreaking painter found inspiration in the faces and bodies of the humble people he encountered on Rome's streets. His canvasses offer stunning visual confirmation of the central place of ordinary denizens in a full portrait of life in Renaissance Rome. In the excerpt, Bellori notes specifically The Fortune Teller *(ca. 1594) and* Penitent Magdalene *(ca. 1594–1595) in this regard. Another early biographer, Giulio Mancini, noted the even more controversial mixing of street life and art in Caravaggio's hotly contested* Death of the Virgin *(1604–1606), in which he used an easily recognized local prostitute as a model for the Virgin Mary.*

The second document is an inventory of Caravaggio's household possessions, taken in the context of a legal dispute that occurred shortly before he fled Rome in the spring of 1606 to escape a murder charge, as described later in the Bellori excerpt. From such mundane listings,

Howard Hibbard and Shirley G. Hibbard, *Caravaggio* (New York: Westview Press, 1985), 361–62, 364–65, 367–70; Maurizio Marini and Sandro Corradini, "Inventarium omnium et singulorum bonorum mobilium di Michelangelo da Caravaggio 'pittore,'" in *Artibus et Historiae*, 14, n. 28 (1993), 161–76.

historians of material culture are able to gauge accurately the circum-
stances in which Renaissance people of modest means lived.

A Biography

[Michele Caravaggio] went to Rome, where he lived without lodgings
and without provisions; since models, without which he did not know
how to paint, were too expensive, he did not earn enough to pay his
expenses. Michele was therefore forced by necessity to work for Cavalier Giuseppe d'Arpino, who had him paint flowers and fruit, which he
imitated so well that from then on they began to attain that greater
beauty that we love today. He painted a vase of flowers sprinkled with
the transparencies of the water and glass and the reflections of a window of the room, rendering flowers with the freshest dewdrops; and
he painted other excellent pictures of similar imitations. But he worked
reluctantly at these things and felt deep regret at not being able to paint
figures. When he met Prospero, a painter of grotesques, he took the
opportunity to leave Giuseppe in order to compete with him for the
glory of painting. Then he began to paint according to his own inclina-
tions; not only ignoring but even despising the superb statuary of antiquity and the famous paintings of Raphael, he considered nature to be
the only subject fit for his brush. As a result, when he was shown the
most famous statues of Phidias and Glykon in order that he might use
them as models, his only answer was to point toward a crowd of people,
saying that nature had given him an abundance of masters. And to give
authority to his words, he called a gypsy who happened to pass by in
the street and, taking her to his lodgings, he portrayed her in the act of
predicting the future, as is the custom of these Egyptian women [*The
Fortune Teller*, ca. 1594]. He painted a young man who places his gloved
hand on his sword and offers the other hand bare to her, which she
holds and examines; and in these two half-figures Michele captured the
truth so purely as to confirm his beliefs. A similar story is told about the
ancient painter Eupompos—though this is not the time to discuss to
what extent such teachings are praiseworthy. Since Caravaggio aspired
only to the glory of color, so that the complexion, skin, blood, and natural surfaces might appear real, he directed his eye and work solely to
that end, leaving aside all the other aspects of art. Therefore, in order to
find figure types and to compose them, when he came upon someone in
town who pleased him he made no attempt to improve on the creations
of nature. He painted a girl drying her hair, seated on a little chair with

her hands in her lap [*Penitent Magdalene*, ca. 1594–1595]. He portrayed her in a room, adding a small ointment jar, jewels and gems on the floor, pretending that she is the Magdalen. She holds her head a little to one side, and her cheek, neck, and breast are rendered in pure, simple, and true colors, enhanced by the simplicity of the whole figure, with her arms covered by a blouse and her yellow gown drawn up to her knees over a white underskirt of flowered damask. We have described this figure in detail in order to show his naturalistic style and the way in which he imitates truthful coloration by using only a few hues. . . .

The painters then in Rome were greatly taken by this novelty, and the young ones particularly gathered around him, praised him as the unique imitator of nature, and looked on his work as miracles. They outdid each other in imitating his works, undressing their models and raising their lights. Without devoting themselves to study and instruction, each one easily found in the piazza and in the street their masters and the models for imitating nature. With this easy style attracting the others, only the older painters already set in their styles were dismayed by this new study of nature: they never stopped attacking Caravaggio and his style, saying that he did not know how to come out of the cellar and that, lacking *invenzione* and *disegno* [imagination and technique], without decorum or art, he painted all his figures with a single source of light and on one plane without any diminution; but such accusations did not stop the flight of his fame.

Caravaggio painted the portrait of Cavalier [Giambattista] Marino, with the reward of praise from literary men; the names of both the painter and the poet were sung in Academies; in fact Marino in particular so praised the head of Medusa by Caravaggio that Cardinal Del Monte gave it to the Grand Duke of Tuscany. Because of his kindness and his delight in Caravaggio's style, Marino introduced the painter into the house of Monsignor Melchiorre Crescenzi, clerk of the papal chamber. Michele painted the portrait of this most learned prelate and another one of Virgilio Crescenzi who, as heir of Cardinal Contarelli, chose him to compete with Giuseppino [Cesari d'Arpino] for the paintings in the chapel of San Luigi dei Francesi. Marino, who was the friend of both painters, suggested that Giuseppe, an expert fresco painter, be given the figures on the wall above and Michele the oil paintings. Here something happened that greatly upset Caravaggio with respect to his reputation. After he had finished the central picture of St. Matthew and installed it on the altar, the priests took it down, saying that the figure with its legs crossed and its feet rudely exposed to the public had neither decorum nor the appearance of a saint. Caravaggio was in despair at such an outrage over his first work in a church, when Marchese Vincenzo Giustiniani acted in his favor and freed him from this predicament. . . .

But Caravaggio's preoccupation with painting did not calm his restless nature. After having painted for a few hours in the day he used to go out on the town with his sword at his side, like a professional swordsman, seeming to do anything but paint. And during a tennis match with a young friend of his, they began hitting each other with their rackets. At the end he drew his sword, killed the young man, and was also wounded himself. Fleeing from Rome, without money and being followed, he found refuge in Zagarolo under the protection of Duke Marzio Colonna, where he painted Christ in Emmaus between the Apostles and another half-figure of Magdalen. . . .

In order to free himself he was exposed to grave danger, but he managed to scale the prison walls at night and to flee unrecognized to Sicily, with such speed that no one could catch him. In Syracuse he painted the altarpiece for the church of Santa Lucia in the port outside the city. He painted the dead St. Lucy blessed by the bishop; there are also two men who dig her grave with shovels. He then went to Messina, where he painted the Nativity for the Capuchin Fathers. It represents the Virgin and Child before a broken-down shack with its boards and rafters apart. St. Joseph leans on his staff, with some shepherds in adoration. For the same Fathers he painted St. Jerome, who is writing in a book, and in the Lazzari Chapel, in the church of the Ministri degl'Infermi, he painted the Resurrection of Lazarus who, being raised from the sepulchre, opens his arms as he hears the voice of Christ who calls him and extends his hand toward him. Martha is crying and Magdalen appears astonished, and there is a figure who puts his hand to his nose to protect himself from the stink of the corpse. The painting is huge, and the figures are in a grotto with brilliant light on the nude body of Lazarus and those who support him. This painting is very highly esteemed for its powerful realism. But misfortune did not abandon Michele, and fear hunted him from place to place. Consequently he hurried across Sicily and from Messina went to Palermo, where he painted another Nativity for the Oratorio of San Lorenzo. The Virgin is shown adoring her newborn child, with St. Francis, St. Lawrence, the seated St. Joseph, and above an angel in the air. The lights are diffused among shadows in the darkness.

After this he no longer felt safe in Sicily, and so he departed the island and sailed back to Naples, where he thought he would stay until he got word of his pardon allowing him to return to Rome. And hoping to placate the Grand Master [of the Knights Hospitaller, Friar Alof de Wignacourt], Caravaggio sent to him as a present a half-figure of Herodias with the head of St. John the Baptist in a basin. These efforts did not succeed. Indeed, one day at the doorway of the Osteria del Ciriglio he was surrounded by armed men who attacked him and wounded him in the face. Thus, as soon as possible, although suffering the fiercest pain, he boarded a *felucca* and headed for Rome, having by then obtained his freedom from the pope through the intercession of Cardinal Gonzaga. Upon his arrival ashore, a Spanish guard, who was waiting for another knight, arrested him by mistake, holding him prisoner. And when he was finally released he never again saw his *felucca* or his possessions. Thus, in a miserable state of anxiety and desperation, he ran along the beach in the heat of the summer sun. Arriving at Porto Ercole, he collapsed and was seized by a malignant fever that killed him in a few days, at about forty years of age, in 1609. This was a sad year for painting, since Annibale Carracci and Federico Zuccaro also died. Thus Caravaggio ended his life on a deserted beach while in Rome people were enthusiastically waiting for his return.

Inventory of Caravaggio's Possessions in Vicolo di San Biagio, Rome, August 26, 1605

This is the inventory of all the movable effects of the painter Michelangelo da Caravaggio, which were found. . . .

First, a kitchen dresser made of white poplar wood, with three compartments and an alder frame, containing eleven pieces of glassware, namely glasses, carafes and straw flasks, a plate, two salt shakers, three spoons, a chopping board and a bowl, and on the above-mentioned dresser two brass candlesticks, another plate, two small knives and three terracotta vases.

Item a water jug.
Two stools.
Item a red table with two drawers.
Item a couple of bedside tables. A picture.
Item a small coffer covered with black leather, containing a pair of
    ragged breeches and a jacket.
A guitar, a violin.
A dagger, a pair of earrings, a worn-out belt and a door leaf.
Item a rather big table.
Item two old straw chairs and a small broom.
Item two swords, and two hand daggers.
Item a pair of green breeches.

Item a mattress. Item a shield. Item a blanket.
Item a foldaway bed to be used for servants.
Item a bedstead with two posts.
Item a chamber-pot.
Item a stool. Item an old chest.
Item a majolica basin.
Item another chest containing twelve books.
Item two large pictures to paint.
Item a chest containing certain rags.
Item three stools. Item a large mirror. Item a mirrored shield
    [convex mirror].
Item three other smaller pictures.
Item a small three-legged table.
Item three large stretchers. Item a large wooden canvas.
Item an ebony chest containing a knife.
Item two bedside tables.
Item a tall wooden tripod.
Item a small cart with some papers with [test] colors.
Item a halberd. Item two more stretchers.

11

ARTEMISIA GENTILESCHI

Testimony

1612

*This document contains extracts from the summary transcript of a trial
for rape held in a Roman papal court. The circumstances revealed
during the criminal process tell us much about the vulnerability of
women, in this case a young woman of well-to-do circumstances, in the
world of Renaissance men.*

Mary D. Garrard, *Artemisia Gentileschi: The Image of the Female Hero in Italian
Baroque Art* (Princeton, N.J.: Princeton University Press, 1989), 415–16.

*As a teenager, the aspiring artist Artemisia Gentileschi, daughter of
the prominent painter Orazio Gentileschi, was raped by Agostino Tassi,
a Tuscan painter hired by her father. Orazio had employed Agostino
primarily to collaborate on Orazio's lucrative commissions and second-
arily as a tutor for his promising daughter (since women were denied
admission to official schools for painters). Several months elapsed before
the rape was reported to authorities, and Artemisia freely testified at
the eventual trial that during this time Agostino repeatedly promised
to marry her, so she engaged freely in loving sexual relations with him.
Later, Orazio, angered over Agostino's purported theft of a painting,
petitioned Pope Paul V (1605–1621) requesting a church trial against
Agostino and his accomplice on charges of having raped Artemisia.
Some interpreters offer an alternate explanation of the delay, suggesting
that Orazio went to court as soon as he found out about his daughter's
relations with Agostino or when he realized that Agostino was not about
to marry Artemisia. While the evidence does not provide certainty about
motivation, by not calling for a public trial until many months after the
rape, Orazio put revenge ahead of any regard for his daughter's welfare
or reputation. Caught in a hopeless trap, Artemisia obeyed her father and
testified voluntarily about what had happened, subsequently undergoing a
court-ordered gynecological examination and torture with thumbscrews to
test her veracity.*

*Further court investigation revealed that Agostino previously had been
married in Florence, had committed adulterous incest, and was a suspect
in his now-deceased wife's death. In his defense, Agostino charged that
Artemisia was a woman of loose morals who had posed nude for male
artists and that Orazio had pimped her. The record of the trial's outcome
has never been located, but we do know that Agostino stayed in the papal
prison of Tor di Nona for another eight months and then was released.*

*The graphic quality of Artemisia's testimony may be shocking,
although the specifics of rape were no different for a Renaissance victim
than they are for women today (and as such, are not necessary to include
in full detail in the excerpt provided below). Artemisia Gentileschi over-
came her ordeal, married and gave birth to several children, and went on
to enjoy a highly successful career as an artist in Florence, Naples, and
the court of Charles I in England. She was estranged from her father for a
number of years, but eventually they did work jointly on various commissions. Art critics note that in her best-known and often repeated painting
of Judith Beheading Holofernes, she used herself as the model for Judith,
and Holofernes looks remarkably like Agostino Tassi.*

While I was at home, the parish Fathers dropped by to pick up the holy cards for Communion and left the door open. With that, Agostino took the opportunity to come into the house and, on seeing those Fathers, began to boast that he could beat them up, speaking to himself so that they couldn't hear him. Then he left, but as soon as the Fathers had gone, he came back to complain that I behaved badly towards him and that I didn't care about him, saying that I would regret it. And I answered: "Regret what, regret what? He who wants me must give me this," meaning marry me and put a ring on my finger. I turned my back on him and went to my room and he left. On the same day, after I had eaten lunch, as it was a rainy day, I was painting an image of one of [her maidservant] Tuzia's boys for my own pleasure. Agostino stopped by and managed to come in because the masons who were working in the house had left the door open. When he found me painting, he said: "Not so much painting, not so much painting," and he grabbed the palette and brushes from my hands and threw them around, saying to Tuzia: "Get out of here." And when I said to Tuzia not to go and not to leave me, as I had previously signaled to her, she said: "I don't want to stay here and argue, I want to go about my own business." Before she left, Agostino put his head on my breast, and as soon as she was gone he took my hand and said: "Let's walk together a while, because I hate sitting down."

While we walked two or three times around the room I told him that I was feeling ill and I thought I had a fever. He replied; "I have more of a fever than you do." After we had walked around two or three times, each time going by the bedroom door, when we were in front of the bedroom door, he pushed me in and locked the door. He then threw me onto the edge of the bed, pushing me with a hand on my breast, and he put a knee between my thighs to prevent me from closing them. Lifting my clothes, which he had a great deal of trouble doing, he placed a hand with a handkerchief at my throat and on my mouth to keep me from screaming. . . .

And after he had done his business he got off me. When I saw myself free, I went to the table drawer and took a knife and moved toward Agostino saying: "I'd like to kill you with this knife because you have dishonored me." He opened his coat and said: "Here I am," and I threw the knife at him, and he shielded himself; otherwise I would have hurt him and might easily have killed him. However, I wounded him slightly on the chest and some blood came out, only a little since I had barely touched him with the point of the knife. And the said Agostino then fastened his coat. I was crying and suffering over the wrong he had done me, and to pacify me, he said: "Give me your hand, I promise to marry you as soon as I get out of the labyrinth I am in." He added: "I warn you that when I take you [as my wife] I don't want any foolishness [unfaithfulness on her part]," and I answered: "I think you will see if there is any foolishness." And with this good promise I felt calmer, and with this promise he induced me later on to yield lovingly, many times, to his desires, since many times he has also reconfirmed this promise to me. When later I heard that he had a wife I reproached him about this betrayal, and he always denied it, telling me he didn't have a wife, and he always reaffirmed that no one but himself had had me. This is all that happened between Agostino and me.

3

Renaissance Visitors

12

WILLIAM THOMAS

The History of Italy

1549

William Thomas (ca. 1507–1554) was the first Englishman since Geoffrey Chaucer (ca. 1342–1400) to show serious interest in the Italian language. His brief history of Italy heralded the British fascination with things Italian in general and with Rome in particular that blossomed in the Elizabethan era and continues to the present day. His role as a catalyst in England's admiration for Italian culture (and sunny climate) may seem odd, given his anti-Catholic beliefs. His strong Protestant leanings led to his being hanged in England in 1554 for his part in the Wyatt conspiracy, a rebellion sparked by fears of the nation's re-Catholicization should Queen Mary wed Philip II.

Before coming to Italy in 1545 or 1546 for a stay that lasted three years, he had been convicted of embezzlement to cover gambling debts and then pardoned. Apparently he lived off money from his parents while visiting numerous Italian cities, writing an Italian grammar book, and reading profusely in preparation for his History of Italy. *He viewed Rome through his strong distaste for the ostentatious ceremonial celebrations of Catholicism. Yet his enchantment with the city and its people sparkles between the lines, and his book reads like a historical introduction to a travel guide meant to encourage his fellow countrymen to follow in his footsteps.*

William Thomas, *The History of Italy* (Ithaca, N.Y.: Cornell University Press, 1963), 45–53.

Of the ground contained within the walls scarcely the third part is now inhabited, and that not where the beauty of Rome hath been but for the most part on the plain to the waterside and in the Vatican, because that since the Bishops began to reign every man hath coveted to build as near the court as might be. Nevertheless, those streets and buildings that are there at this time are so fair that I think no city doth excel it, by reason they have had the beautifullest things of the antiquities before rehearsed to garnish their houses withal, specially the Bishop, his cardinals, prelates, and other members of his church, who have all at their commandment. For though the Romans have in their hearts unto this day a certain memory of their ancient liberty, which they have attempted many times to recover, yet doth the Bishop keep them in such subjection that they dare not once stir for their lives, but speak they may what they list, so it be no treason; and therefore many times you shall hear them rail on the Bishop and his officers that it is a wonder. In effect, the present state of Rome in comparison of the ancient state deserveth not to be spoken of, and yet I believe that in the Romans' most glory there was never half so much pomp used as now. O what a world it is to see the pride and abomination that the churchmen there maintain! What is a king? what is an emperor in his majesty? anything like to the Roman Bishop? No, surely no; I would not wish them so to be. And to the intent you may the better perceive it, you shall understand that on Christmas Day the year of our Lord 1547, Paul the Third being Bishop, I noted his coming to church because it was a principal feast celebrated *in pontificalibus*. Wherefore early in the morning I resorted to the palace and there waited the coming of the cardinals, that for the most part lie in the city and to come to St. Peter's must pass Ponte Sant' Angelo; where is an old order that whensoever any cardinal passeth the bridge there is a piece of ordnance shot off in the castle for an honor that the Bishop is bound to observe towards his brethren.

I had not been long in the palace but I heard two pieces shot off at once, whereby I knew that two cardinals were coming, and therefore resorted to the gate to see them and their train.

From Castel Sant' Angelo to St. Peter's stairs there is an exceeding fair street, straight and level more than a quarter of a mile long, called *Borgo San Pietro*; in the further end whereof I saw these cardinals come, and therewith out of the Bishop's palace came his guard of Switzers all in white harness and there alongst before the gate made a lane half on one side and half on the other, with their two drums and a fife before them. And as soon as the cardinals approached, the drums and fife began to play and so continued till the cardinals were well entered amongst the guard. Then the trumpets blew up another while till the cardinals were almost at the gate, and as they should enter, the shawms [a musical instrument similar to an oboe] began to play and ceased not till they were alighted and mounted up the stairs to the Bishop's lodging.

The like ceremonies were used unto all the cardinals that came, whether one came alone or many together. And there [I] tarried more than two hours, hearkening to this gunshot and merry piping, and reckoned above forty cardinals that came thus riding, sometime one alone and sometime three or four together.

There was no cardinal that came without a great train of gentlemen and prelates, well horsed and appointed some had forty, some fifty, and some sixty or more and next before every of them rode two henchmen, the one carrying a cushion and a rich cloth, and the other a pillar of silver; and the cardinals themselves, appareled in robes of crimson charnlet with red hats on their heads, rode on mules.

When they were all come to the palace and had waited awhile in the chamber of presence, the Bishop himself, with the three-crowned miter full of jewels, in a very rich cope, with shoes of crimson velvet set with precious stones, and in all his other pontifical apparel, came forth and at the chamber door sat him down in a chair of crimson velvet, through the which runneth two staves covered with the same. Thus being set, the prelates and clergy with the other officers passed on afore him; which are such a number as were able to make the muster of a battle if they were well ordered in the field: dataries, treasurers, clerks of the chamber, penitentiaries, prebendaries, notaries, protonotaries, and a thousand more, each order of them in his divers device of parliament robes, all in scarlet and for the most part finely furred. Then came the double cross, the sword, and the imperial hat, and after that the cardinals by two and two, and between every two a great rout of gentlemen. Then came the ambassadors and next them the Bishop himself, blessing all the way and carried in his chair by eight men, clothed in long robes of scarlet; and on either side of him went his guard, making room and crying, *Abbasso, Abbasso,* for they that will not willingly kneel shall be made [to] kneel by force. And I think verily the foremost of this order was distant from the hindermost more than a quarter of a mile.

Thus when he came into the midst of the church against the sacrament of the altar, he turned himself towards it and, bowing his head a little, seemed to make a certain familiar reverence. Then was he carried into the chapel, brought behind the altar (for the altar standeth in the midst, open every way), and there in a throne of wonderful majesty was set up as a god.

The cardinals then bestowed themselves after their ancienity in certain stalls, somewhat lower about the choir. Then sat the ambassadors and other prelates at their feet. And so when they were set, the chapel began the Offertory of the Mass and sang so sweetly that methought I never heard the like. At the communion of the Mass, the cardinal that celebrated brake the host in three pieces, whereof he eat one himself, and the other two he delivered upon the paten to a cardinal appointed that brought it to the Bishop, and in his presence (for fear of poisoning) took assay of the second piece and delivered him the third. When the Mass was finished, the Bishop gave his benediction, with many years of pardon, and then returned to the palace in like order as he came.

As for the pomp he useth when he rideth abroad, I need not to speak of it, considering what I have said, saving that you shall understand how Corpus Domini is always carried in a tabernacle before him on a white hackney that is taught to kneel both at the setting up and also at the taking down of it.

Indeed, the Bishop for his own ordinary keepeth no great house, but his train exceedeth all that I have seen. For every cardinal and prelate keepeth house according to his ability, and some of them are so precise that if one of their retinue be missing when they go out of their doors, be it gentleman or other, he forfeiteth a certain piece of money, which he is constrained forthwith to pay. And lightly there is none of them without three or four pages trimmed like young princes, for what purpose I would be loath to tell.

If I should say that under their long robes they hide the greatest pride of the world, it might happen some men would believe it, but that they are the vainest men of all other their own acts do well declare. For their ordinary pastime is to disguise themselves, to go laugh at the courtesans' houses, and in the shroving time to ride masking about with them; which is the occasion that Rome wanteth no *jolie dames*, specially the street called *Julia*, which is more than half a mile long, fair builded on both sides, in manner inhabited with none other but courtesans, some worth 10 and some worth 20,000 crowns, more or less, as their reputation is. And many times you shall see a courtesan ride into the country with ten or twelve horses waiting on her.

Briefly, by report Rome is not without 40,000 harlots, maintained for the most part by the clergy and their followers. So that the Romans themselves suffer their wives to go seldom abroad, either to church or other place, and some of them scarcely to look out at a lattice window; whereof their proverb saith, *In Roma vale piu la puttana che la moglie*

Romana: that is to say, "In Rome the harlot hath a better life than she that is a Roman's wife."

In their apparel they are as gorgeous as may be and have in their going such a solemn pace as I never saw. In conclusion, to live in Rome is more costly than in any other place, but he that hath money may have there what him liketh.

13

JOACHIM DU BELLAY

The Regrets

1558

Joachim du Bellay (1522–1560) came to Rome in 1553 as household secretary for his father's cousin, the powerful Cardinal Jean du Bellay, and stayed for four-and-a-half years, enjoying full access to all that the city had to offer. In The Regrets *he employs the fourteen-line sonnet form of poetry (4, 4, 3, 3) to express his sorrow over the ruin into which ancient Rome's glorious monuments have fallen. He has little to say about formal Catholic Reformation theology and practice but much to observe about the church itself and about how a person gets by in the city that left him completely disillusioned. In one sonnet he even seems to welcome the destruction that a recurrence of an event such as the 1527 sack of Rome might bring. His reminiscences contrast sharply with the warm memories of Roman sojourns expressed by other visitors, such Erasmus (Document 21). Shortly after returning to France, du Bellay died of an apparent stroke at the age of thirty-seven, leaving behind several volumes of exquisite poetry that have earned him a leading place in French Renaissance literature. The people he addresses in the various sonnets are friends, influential patrons, and fellow French writers.*

Joachim du Bellay, *The Regrets: A Bilingual Edition*, trans. and ed. David R. Slavitt (Evanston, Ill.: Northwestern University Press, 2004), 137, 171, 175, 179, 181, 213, 219, 247.

Sonnet 61

A friend of the heart, they say, should be a friend
of the purse. But *they* are the ones who try to borrow
other people's money, and on the morrow
will be in the workhouse or come to an even worse end

in the river. But think: however abundant the spring,
it can exhaust itself, and a rich man can be
a borrower one day, having been so free
and open-handed. It's a most dangerous thing

you're doing, [Jean-Antoine de Simiane] Gordes. In Rome, if you
    want to last,
you must teach yourself to be slow with your purse and fast
with fair words that can win you friends on the cheap.

Dipping into your pocket, all that you do
is put at risk the gold and the friendship, too,
both of which you might have been able to keep.

Sonnet 78

Bologna, Venice, Padua, and Ferrara
I will not speak about, or Naples or
Milan, or which is best set up for war,
or which is best for a shopping spree or for a

holiday, but I'll write of this antic scene
in Rome, the church's headquarters, where under
the triple crown there is hatred, ambition (no wonder!),
pride, and pretense, and generous men and mean,

and learned and stupid rub shoulders, as virtue and vice
saunter through the piazzas together. It's nice,
the way they get on together here. Praying and sinning

can mix together, dear [Jacques] Pelletier [du Mans], as we're told
the elements did in the tohu-and-bohu [Genesis 1.2] of old
in that Chaos they say obtained at the world's beginning.

Sonnet 80

Whenever I go to the Vatican, I see
pride, vice in disguise, pomp on display

to the beating of massed drums, and every way
I look, rich scarlet habits in panoply.

If I go to the bourse, what I find there is also dismal:
expatriate Florentines or the somewhat less
rich Sienese near tears for their unsuccess
as they trade rumors and currencies. It's abysmal

everywhere I go in Rome. There are whores
who beckon bold as brass from open doors,
winking, leering, and ready to jump my bones.

And if I go farther and leave the new Rome behind,
the old Rome's no less depressing: there, I find
its once proud monuments fallen to heaps of stones.

Sonnet 82

You want to know, [Jean] Duthier [Seigneur de Beauregard], what
    kind of place
Rome is? It's the world's great stage, on which is seen
and heard whatever can be or is or has been.
Here is the wheel of Fortune, and this is the place

where one may rise as another falls, and the sins
of each are plain for all to see, however
much he may try to conceal them and however clever
he thinks he is. But everyone knows, and grins.

Rumor travels fast, as the truth does too.
Diplomats have their affairs and courtiers screw,
and everyone is procuring with more or less

boldness and license, and idleness wins out,
unopposed in virtue's all but total rout
that cynical fools discuss in their shamelessness.

Sonnet 83

Do not suppose, dear [Florimond] Robertet [Baron of Alluye], that
    the Rome
of today is at all like the city that you found
so pleasing once. It's changed, decayed, unsound.
Not even making love is the same. We've come

to a sorry state where the music is stilled and the dance
has stopped. The air is vile, and violence
is everywhere. Nothing makes any sense.
There's hunger, suffering, fear. The artisan wants

customers; the lawyer has let his practice
go; the merchant has shut his shop; and the fact is
his children beg on the streets, where nervous men

in uniforms and helmets are out on patrol.
We hear the trumpets' blare and the snare drums' roll
and fear—or hope—for Rome to be sacked again.

Sonnet 99

I wander through the streets here where people abound—
priests and prelates, a banker, a monk in black,
and after a while, I begin to notice the lack
of what one would see in Paris—no women around!

One would think, after Noah's flood, that Rome
had not quite been restored and God had merely
restocked half of the world. The custom, here, clearly,
is that wives and daughters of gentlemen stay at home.

The only women one sees on the streets are those
who walk the streets, the hookers in garish clothes.
And after a while one accepts this as normal. I fear

when I get home again, there's a good chance
it may take me time to readjust, and in France,
I'll treat the women as I have learned to do here.

Sonnet 102

They warn you not to take wooden nickels, but here
they can take a block of wood, or a blockhead
and make him a pope or cardinal robed in red,
and three days later, nobody thinks it's queer.

Princes and kings are used to grandeur and show,
which do not, therefore, drive them crazy, but these
so suddenly promoted nonentities
are dazzled by it. I have seen great men go

alone through the streets of Rome whose names strike awe
in every person's heart and whose word is law.
That happens. What is harder to explain

is how it befalls that one of these upstarts passes,
whose father, a plowman, stared into his oxen's asses,
preceded by pages and followed now by a train.

Sonnet 116

Let us get out, Dilliers [a friend, not further identified], while we
    can. Let's fly
at once from this grasping town and inhumane
people, before the furious deities rain
down on our heads their thunderbolts from on high.

Mars is let loose, and the doors of the temple of war
are opened wide, as the high priest of Rome pursues
the German heretics and the Spanish Jews,
those converts — Marranos who pray to God as before.

There are soldiers everywhere, and trumpets and drums.
A platoon marches down one street, and another comes
on horseback up another. The prospects are dark.

All you hear now is the talk of blood and fire,
and how the situation grows ever more dire.
Can the pope, our captain, save the Roman ark?

14

ANTHONY MUNDAY

The English Roman Life

1581

In The English Roman Life, *Anthony Munday (1560–1633) provides a tell-all about the English Catholic College (Seminary) in Rome. He stayed there in 1579 with his friend and traveling companion Thomas Nowell. Munday probably was masquerading as a Catholic, whereas Nowell seriously studied for the priesthood until he was declared unsuitable and dismissed from the seminary in 1583. Both men turned virulently antipapal in the years that followed—Munday publicly with this book and Nowell privately as a spy on behalf of Protestant groups in England. Historians of English anti-Catholicism have shown suitable interest in the precise moment of Munday's confessional turnaround, but his work is particularly noteworthy for its observations on what he saw outside the English seminary's confines.*

Munday's sightings are thoroughly iconoclastic and hostile to Rome's ruling elite. He offers an account of abuses directed against the city's Jews during Carnivale, and the intensity and sheer disgust in his descriptions of popular devotional practices match those in Luther's Table Talk *(Document 22). Ordinary Renaissance Romans did not feel as disgusted. For those forming the base of Rome's social pyramid, the ritualistic quality and affirmation of barriers in these ceremonies provided a measure of emotional solidarity. To put the matter bluntly, Christians enjoyed shaming and ridiculing excluded groups such as Jews, and this document provides no evidence that they had serious qualms about doing so.*

Anthony Munday, *The English Roman Life* (London: John Charlwoode, 1590), 28–30, 61–64. Spelling and punctuation have been modernized. See also Philip J. Ayres, ed., *Anthony Munday. The English Roman Life* (Oxford, U.K.: Clarendon Press, 1980), for the 1582 edition, esp. the introductory material, xiii–xxviii; more generally, see Donna B. Hamilton, *Anthony Munday and the Catholics, 1560–1633* (Aldershot, U.K.: Ashgate, 2005).

In St. John Lateran's Church

As we come first to the little chapels before the church (wherein they say, Our Lady has been diverse times seen: and therefore has left such holiness there, as they pray there a good while) there stands a round pillar of stone, seeming to be but lately made: on this stone, say they, the cock stood and crowed at what time Peter denied Christ: and therefore they do use to kiss it, make courtesy to it, and rub their [rosary] beads on it.

Near to this stone is a broad gate, being the entrance into the aforesaid chapels, and on the one side of this gate there is two round rings of iron, whereon sometime a gate has been hanged, to open and shut: in these rings, say they, the Jews did stick banners all the while that Christ was crucified, and therefore for the holiness of them, they will draw their beads through the said rings, and kiss them when they have done.

From there we go to a fair large place, in the midst whereof stands a font, wherein they say, Constantinus Magnus was christened: in this font every year on Easter even they do christen Jews, such as do change to their religion. For there is a certain place appointed for sermons, whereat the Jews whether they will or no must be present, because one of their own rabbis preaches to them, to convert them, as himself has been a great while.

In Rome, the Jews have a dwelling place within themselves, being locked in their streets by gates on either side, and the Romans every night keep the keys: all the day time they go abroad in the city, and will buy the oldest apparel that is, an old cloak, doublet, or hose, that a man would think not worth a penny, of the Jews you may have the quantity of four or five shillings for them. Now, that the Jews may be known from any other people, everyone wears a yellow cap or hat, and if he go abroad without it they will use him very ill favouredly.

In this order they come to the sermon, and when any of them does change his faith: he takes his yellow cap or hat off from his head, and throws it away with great violence; then will a hundred offer him a black cap or a hat; and greatly rejoice that they have so won him. All his riches he then must forsake, that goes to the Pope's use, being one of his shifts: and to this aforesaid font he is brought, clothed all in white, a white cap, a white cloak, and everything white about him, with a holy candle burning, that he bears in his hand. Then is he there baptized by an Englishman, who is named Bishop Goldwell, sometime the Bishop of St. Asaph in Wales: he has this office, makes all the English priests in the College, and lives there among the Theatines [a Catholic Reformation order of priests, founded 1524] very pontifically. After the Jews be thus baptized, they be brought into the church, and there they see the hallowing of the Paschal, which is a mighty great wax taper; and then a device wherein is enclosed a number of squibs is shot off, when throughout all the church they cry, "*Sic transit gloria mundi* [Thus passes the glory of the world]." From there they go to a college which the Pope has erected for such Jews as in this manner turn to his religion: there they stay a certain time, and afterward they be turned out to get their living as they can; none of their former riches they must have again, for that goes to the maintenance of the Pope's pontificality. This aforesaid font is a holy thing, and there must prayers be likewise said. . . .

Of the *Carne-vale* in Rome: the Pope's General Cursing on *Maundy* [Holy] *Thursday* [before Easter]: and the Manner of the *Flagellante* That Night

CHAPTER 7

During the time of Shrovetide, there is in Rome kept a very great coil,[1] which they use to call the Carne-vale, which endures the space of three or four days, all which time the Pope keeps himself out of Rome, so great is the noise and hurly-burly. The gentlemen will attire themselves in diverse forms of apparel, some like women, others like Turks, and every one almost in a contrary order of disguising; and either they be on horseback, or in coaches, none of them on foot, for the people that stand on the ground to see this pastime are in very great danger of their lives, by reason of the running of coaches and great horses, as never in all my life did I see the like stir. And all this is done where the courtesans be, to show them delight and pastime, for they have coverlets laid out at their windows whereon they stand leaning forth, to receive diverse devices of rosewater, and sweet odors in their faces, which the gentlemen will throw up to their windows.

During this time everyone wears a disguised visor on his face so that no one knows what or whence they be, and if anyone bear a secret malice to another, he may then kill him, and nobody will lay hands on him, for all this time they will obey no law. I saw a brave Roman, who rode there very pleasant in his coach, and suddenly came one who discharged a pistol upon him, yet nobody made any account either of the

---

[1]coil: tumult.

murderer or the slain gentleman: beside, there were diverse slain, both by villainy, and the horses or the coaches, yet they continued on their pastime, making no regard of them.

The first day of their Carne-vale, the Jews in Rome cause an ensign to be placed at the Capitol, where likewise they appoint certain wagers at their own costs; and then they run stark naked from Porta Populo [Popolo] unto the Capitol for them, the which I judge above a mile in length. And all the way they gallop their great horses after them, and carry goads with sharp points of steel in them, wherewith they will prick the Jews on the naked skin, if so be they do not run faster than their horses gallop, so that you shall see some of their backs all on gore blood. Then he that is foremost, and soonest comes to the Capitol, he is set on a horse back without any saddle, one going before him carrying the ensign: but then you shall see a hundred boys, who have provided a number of oranges, they will so pelt the poor Jew, that before he can get up to the Capitol, he will be beaten beside his horse four or five times.

The next day there are certain of the Christians that run naked likewise, but nobody pursues them, either with horse or coach, and the wager they run for, the Jews must pay likewise. Then the buffle [Italian *bufala*] and the ass run, but it is impossible for me to tell all the knavery used about this: and therefore thus much shall suffice of the Carne-vale, letting you understand, that they who were most knavishly disposed in this sport, on Ash Wednesday came to take ashes in such meek order, as though it had never been they.

On Maundy Thursday, the Pope comes into his gallery over St. Peter's, sitting in his chair wherewith he is carried on men's shoulders, and there he has a great painted holy candle in his hand burning, when as a cardinal on each side of him, the one in Latin, the other in Italian, sings the Pope's general malediction. There he curses the Turk, and Her Majesty, our most gracious Princess and governess, affirming her to be far worse than the Turk, or the cruellest tyrant that is. He curses likewise all Calvinians, Lutherans, Zwinglians, and all that are not according to his disposition. When he has cursed all that he can, saying amen, he lets the candle fall: when as the people will scramble for it, and every one catch a little piece if they can, yea, our Englishmen will be as busy as the best; and one of them chanced to get a piece of the wax of the candle, whereof he made such a bragging when he came to the College, as you will not think that he had got a piece of the candle wherewith the Queen of England was cursed, and that he would keep it so long as he lived.

The same night a number of the basest people and most wicked livers that be among the people gather themselves together in companies, as the Company of the Holy Ghost, the Company of Charity, the Company of Death, and suchlike, every company their crucifix before them, their singers following them, on either side a number of burning torches, and thus they go all whipping themselves.

First they go up into the Pope's palace, and then down into St. Peter's Church, which is all adorned with a number of wax lights; and there on the top of an altar stand a couple of cardinals, who show them the holy handkercher [in Catholic tradition, the cloth used by St. Veronica to wipe the crucified Christ's face], or *Vultus sanctus* (which indeed is nothing but a lively painted picture, overshadowed with a couple of fine lawns, and nobody must desire to see it uncovered, because they say nobody is able to endure the brightness of the face; a number have seen it, and have been [none] the worse a great while after), and all the while that both this, and the spear head, is shown they will whip themselves before them very grievously, and give a general clamor thorough the church: "*Misericordia, misericordia, tu autem Domine miserere nobis* [Mercy, mercy, oh Lord have mercy on us]": and in this order they continue almost the whole night. This is the glory of the Pope, the blindness of the people, and the great folly of our Englishmen, to bring themselves within the compass of such wicked order of life.

God continue his loving and fatherly countenance over England; bless and preserve Her Majesty, and her honorable Council: and exercise us all in fear to him, obedience to her, and faithful continual love to our neighbors. Amen.

15

MICHEL EYQUEM DE MONTAIGNE

Travel Journal: Rome

1580–1581

Initially the wealthy Lord Michel Eyquem de Montaigne (1533–1592) left the recording of travel notes to his secretary, but when this man abandoned the task for other duties, the great essayist became his own diarist, which is where this excerpt begins. Montaigne writes that he made the trip to Rome for pleasure and to restore his health, as he suffered greatly from kidney stones and hoped that the waters of Italy's many hot springs would bring him relief. Along with entries about passing his stones, he shares in exquisite and surprising detail what he saw, not only the magnificent and monumental but the extraordinary particulars of ordinary people's behavior. At times he seems almost naïve, such as when he visits a hot spring without bringing a female companion to enhance the pleasures, as elite Romans typically did. On other occasions he reports notorious behavior quite blandly, as in his March 18 description of punishments meted out to men who had engaged in same-sex marriage ceremonies.

Montaigne was a devout Catholic, and none of the suspicion and ridicule that characterize observations by some English, Spanish, and northern European visitors (Documents 12, 13, 14, 20, 21, and 22) are found in his diary. Instead, he expresses keen insights without becoming overly judgmental. But he also invokes comparisons clearly favorable to his native French culture, as when he observes the shallow quality and heavy reliance on ceremony of popular religious devotion in Rome.

On the first day of March I went to the service at the Sistine Chapel. At the high altar the priest who said mass stood beyond the altar with his face turned towards the people, no one being behind him. On this occasion the Pope was present, for he had some days before excluded therefrom the nuns who had hitherto been wont to be present, so as to

W. G. Waters, trans. and ed., *The Journal of Montaigne's Travels in Italy by Way of Switzerland and Germany in 1580 and 1581* (London: John Murray, 1903), II:113–15, 132–38, 140–51, 158–64.

make more room. In their place he installed, by a most excellent regulation, the poor folk who beg about the city. Each one of the cardinals gave twenty crowns in aid of the movement, and very liberal alms were given by other private persons. To their hospital the Pope has given five hundred crowns a month.

In Rome there is a vast amount of private devotion, and many confraternities in which are manifest striking testimonies of piety, but it seems to me that in general there is less devotion than in the better ordered towns of France. They set more store here on ceremonies, in which they go to great lengths. Here I may write what I will with a free conscience, so I will give two illustrations of my meaning. A certain man was with a courtesan, lying in bed and enjoying the full liberty of the situation, when, at the twenty-fourth hour, the *Ave Maria* sounded, and the girl sprang out of bed and knelt down on the floor to say her prayer. Shortly afterwards he was with another, when suddenly the good mother (for these girls are always in the hands of some old bawd whom they call mother or aunt) knocked at the door and, having entered in a transport of rage, tore off from the girl's neck a ribbon from which was hanging a little image of Our Lady, so that it might not be contaminated by the sinful act of the wearer. The young girl showed herself exceedingly penitent, in that she had omitted her customary practice of first removing this image from her person. . . .

The approaches to Rome in almost every case have a barren and uncultivated look, whether through the unfitness of the soil for cultivation, or whether, as seems more likely, through the absence of husbandmen and handicraftsmen in the city. On my journey hither I met divers troops of villagers from the Grisons and Savoy on their way to seek work in the Roman vineyards and gardens, and they told me they gained this wage every year. The city is all for the court and the nobility, everyone adapting himself to the ease and idleness of ecclesiastic surroundings. There are no main streets of trade; what there are would seem small in a small town, palaces and gardens take up all the space. Nothing is to be seen like the Rue de la Harpe or de Saint Denis; I always fancied I must be walking in the Rue de Seine or on the Quai des Augustins at Paris. The aspect of the city differs little whether the day be a feast or a working day. Services go on all through Lent, and the crowds are just as great on a working day as any other, the streets being full of coaches, prelates, and ladies at this season

On the 16th of March, after our return to Rome, I was taken to make trial of the Roman hot baths at St. Mark's, which have the best repute. I underwent a treatment of moderate strength, and, though I went alone, met with all possible respect. The usual custom is to take a lady as companion, who like yourself will be rubbed by the men in attendance. I learned here the composition of the unguent used for removing hair from the skin. It is made of two parts of quick lime and one of arsenic, blended with lye, and will have effect in less than a quarter of an hour after application. On the 17th I was troubled, not insupportably, with colic for five or six hours, and afterwards passed a large stone the shape of a pine kernel. . . .

On the 18th the Portuguese ambassador did homage to the Pope for the kingdom of Portugal, on behalf of King Philip. This same ambassador represented on other occasions the late King of Portugal, and likewise those states of King Philip with which he was at variance [the Low Countries]. On my way back from Saint Peter's I met a certain man who gave me an interesting account of two occurrences. The first was that the Portuguese had done their homage in Passion week, the service being held in the church of Saint John at the Porta Latina; and the second, that in this very same church, several years ago, certain Portuguese had established a very strange confraternity. These were men who joined themselves in matrimony, using the mass and the same religious ceremonies as we use at our weddings, taking the sacrament together, and reading our marriage service. Then they went and lived together after the fashion of married folk. These fanatics declared that the marriage ceremony alone rendered lawful the union of man and woman, and that their own form of union would become equally lawful should it be sanctioned by the ceremonies and mysteries of the Church. Nine or ten Portuguese belonging to this execrable sect were burnt.

I witnessed the homage done by Spain for the kingdom of Portugal. A salvo of artillery was fired from Saint Angelo and from the palace, and the ambassador was escorted by trumpets and drums and the Pope's archers. I did not go inside to be present at the speechmaking and the other ceremonies. The Muscovite ambassador, who sat at a decorated window to behold the procession, remarked that he had been brought there to witness a great gathering; but in his country, when men spoke of troops of horses, they had in mind twenty-five or thirty thousand, wherefore he made light of the show before him. This I heard from a gentleman who was sent to converse with him through an interpreter. On Palm Sunday, in a church where I went for vespers, I saw a child seated in a chair beside the altar clad in a long gown of new blue taffetas, bareheaded, crowned with olive branches, and holding in his hand a lighted candle of white wax. This boy was about fifteen years old, and had just been discharged by the Pope's order from prison, having been sent there for killing another boy. At Saint John Lateran they showed me some transparent marble.

On the next day the Pope visited the seven churches. He wore boots of flesh-color, with a cross of lighter-colored leather upon each boot. He always takes with him a Spanish horse, a hackney, a mule, and a litter, all equipped in the same fashion, but to-day the horse was lacking. His esquire, with two or three pairs of gilded spurs in his hand, awaited him at the foot of Saint Peter's Stairs; but he put the spurs aside and asked for his litter, in which were hanging two red hats of the same sort. . . .

This same day at the church of Saint John Lateran, in place of the ordinary penitancers who may be seen doing their office in most of the churches, Monsignore the Cardinal of Saint Sixtus sat in a corner, and with a long rod, which he held in his hand, touched the heads of all the men who went by, and of the women also, but these he regarded with a smile and a courtesy of manner apportioned to their consequence and beauty.

On the Wednesday in Holy week I visited the Seven Churches with M. de Foix before dinner and spent about five hours in making the round. I know not why some people should profess to be shocked when they hear this or that prelate accused of vicious practices, when these practices are well known. This very day, in the churches of Saint John Lateran and of Santa Croce in Gerusalemme, I saw written in a most prominent place the history of Pope Sylvester II in which the worst is recorded of him. The circuit of the city from the Porta del Popolo to the Porta de S. Paolo, which I made several times, can be accomplished in three or four hours going at foot pace. That part which lies beyond the river may easily be traversed in an hour and a half. Amongst other pleasures which I enjoyed in Rome during Lent, mention must be made of the sermons. There were many excellent preachers, for instance the renegade rabbi who preached to the Jews on Saturday afternoons in the church of the Trinità. Here was always a congregation of sixty Jews who were bound to be present. This preacher had been a famous doctor amongst them, and now he attacked their belief by their own arguments, even out of the mouths of their rabbis and from the words of the Bible. He had admirable skill and knowledge of the subject, and of the languages necessary for the elaboration of the same. There was another who preached before the Pope and cardinals, named Padre Toledo, a man of extraordinary ability in depth of learning, in appositeness of expression, and in mustering of his arguments, and a third who preached at the church of the Jesuits was distinguished for the beauty of the language he used, the two last being members of the Jesuit society.

It is wonderful how great is the part occupied by this College in the Christian economy, and my belief is that never before has there existed any confraternity which has risen to such eminence, or which may sway so powerfully the destinies of the world, supposing that it should be able to prosecute its designs in the future. It occupies well-nigh the whole of Christendom; it is a nursery of men distinguished in every department of high affairs, and the institution of our Church which the heretics of our day have most to fear.

One of the preachers declared that people nowadays use their coaches as places whence they spy upon their fellows. The habit which the Romans most affect is that of walking about the streets, but as a rule they only rouse themselves to issue forth for the sake of sauntering along from one street to another, without design of going anywhere in particular, one or two of the streets being especially affected for this purpose. In sooth, the chief pleasure to be got from this practice is the sight of the ladies, and especially the courtesans, who exhibit themselves behind their lattices with such refinement of trickery that I have often wondered at the address they display in attracting men's eyes. Often I have got down from my horse and induced some of these ladies to admit me, and have wondered how it was they contrived to make themselves appear so much handsomer than they really were. They have the art of letting a beholder distinguish them by whatever trait of theirs is most seemly; they will let you see only the upper part of the face, or the lower, or the side, veiling and unveiling according to the particular style of countenance, so that an ugly woman is never to be seen at a window. Each one takes her position there for the purpose of saluting and bowing to her acquaintances, who, as they go by, throw up many a glance. An extra privilege, granted to any gallant who may have paid one crown or four for passing the night in a house of this character, is that he is allowed to salute his inamorata in public the next day. Many ladies of quality also show themselves, but it is very easy to perceive that these are of totally different carriage and fashion. This phase of life is best seen from horseback, a usage which is followed by poor wretches like myself, or by young men riding great horses, which they manage with much skill. People of quality never go abroad except in coaches of the most costly sort, and, in order to have a clear view upwards, the roofs of the coaches are fitted with small windows. It was to these windows that the preacher aforesaid alluded when he spoke of the spying which went on in coaches.

On the morning of Holy Thursday the Pope, in pontifical garb, accompanied by the cardinals, repaired to the second platform of the great portico of Saint Peter's bearing a lighted torch in his hand. Then a canon of Saint Peter's, who stood on one side of the balcony, read in a loud voice a bull written in Latin by which men of an infinite variety of sorts and conditions were excommunicated; amongst others the Huguenots were specially named, and all those princes who keep hold on any of the lands of the Church, an article which caused loud laughter from the Cardinals Medici and Carafa, who stood close to the Pope. The reading of this bull lasted a good hour; for when the canon had finished reading an article in Latin, the Cardinal Gonzaga, who stood on the opposite side—uncovered like the canon—would repeat the same in Italian. When the reading was done the Pope cast the lighted torch down amongst the people; and, whether out of jest or not, Cardinal Gonzaga threw down another, three torches having been kindled. This having fallen amongst the people caused a vast disturbance below, everyone scrambling to pick up a fragment of the torch, and giving and taking shrewd blows with fist or cudgel. During the reading of this sentence the balustrade of the portico in front of the Pope was covered with a large piece of black taffetas; but, the excommunication having been pronounced, they folded up this black covering and disclosed one of a different color, whereupon the Pope gave his public blessing.

On these days they exhibit the handkerchief of Saint Veronica. This is a countenance wrought in needlework, of a dark and somber tint, and framed after the fashion of a mirror. It is shown with great ceremony from a high pulpit, five or six paces in width, and the priest who holds it wears on his hands red gloves, while two or three other priests assist him in displaying it. No spectacle provokes such great show of reverence as this, the people all prostrate themselves on the ground, the greater part of them weeping and uttering cries of pity. A woman, whom they declared to be possessed, made a great uproar at the sight of this effigy, and began to screech, and twist her arms, and throw them about. The priests moved round the pulpit and exhibited the effigy, now from one side and now from another, and at every fresh display the people who beheld it cried out aloud. On these same occasions they show to the people likewise with equal ceremonies a lance head enclosed in a crystal vessel. This display is made several times during the day, and the crowd which comes to witness the same is so vast that, as far as the eye can reach from the pulpit aforesaid outside the church, there is nought to be seen but an endless crowd of men and women. Here is the true papal court; the pomp of Rome and its chief grandeur lies in the outward show of religion: and it is a fine sight in these days, this unbounded ardor of the people for their faith. . . .

On the Wednesday after Easter M. Maldonat [Juan Maldonado, a Jesuit theologian], who was then at Rome, inquired of me what might be my opinion of the ways and habits of the city, especially with respect to religion. It happened that our views agreed exactly, to wit, that the common people were beyond comparison more devout in France than in Rome, while the contrary might be affirmed of the richer classes, and especially of those about the court. He told me that whenever he heard men maintain that France was altogether given over to heresy — and especially when the disputants were Spaniards, of whom there were great number in his society — he always answered that more truly religious men might be found in Paris alone than in the whole of Spain. . . .

Then there are always sermons to be listened to at all seasons, or disputes in theology; or again diversion may be found with some courtesan or other, but in this case I found one disadvantage, to wit, that these ladies charge as extortionately for the privilege of simple conversation (which was what I sought, desiring to hear them talk, and to take part in their play of wit) as for the supreme favor, and are just as niggard thereof. All these recreations kept me free effectually from melancholy, which is the death of me, and of irritability, with which I was troubled neither without doors nor within. Thus I found Rome a very pleasant place of sojourn, and I might go on to show that, if I had penetrated more deeply into the inner life of the place, I might have been still more pleased; for I must admit that, though I used all possible care and ingenuity, I only gathered acquaintance with the public aspect of the city, the same that she shows to the meanest stranger.

On Low Sunday I witnessed the ceremony of the bestowal of alms on certain young maidens. On this day the Pope had, in addition to his ordinary equipage, twenty-five horses led before him, decked and covered with cloth of gold, and most richly caparisoned, and ten or twelve mules covered with crimson velvet, all these being led by his lackeys on foot. Then came the Pope's litter, also covered with crimson velvet. The Pope himself rode on his mule, and before him went four men on horseback who carried each one a cardinal's hat, set on the top of a staff which was covered with red velvet and gilt about the handle and the top. The cardinals who followed rode also on mules and wore their pontifical garb, the skirts of their robes being fastened by pins to the mules' bridles. The maidens numbered a hundred and seven, each one being accompanied by an elderly kinswoman, and when the mass was finished they left the church and marched in a long procession. Having re-entered the church of La Minerva — where this function takes place — they passed one by one through the choir and kissed the feet of the Pope; who, after blessing them, gave them each from his own hand a purse of white damask containing a note on his bankers. It was understood that all these girls have found husbands, wherefore they come to ask for a dowry, which is fixed at a sum of thirty-five crowns apiece, in addition to the white robe costing five crowns, which they wear at their wedding. Their faces were covered with linen veils, with no opening save holes to look through.

I was speaking lately of the advantages of Rome, and will now add, in reference to this matter, that I find it, of all towns in the world, the one most filled with the corporate idea, in which difference of nationality counts least; for, by its very nature, it is a patchwork of strangers, each one being as much at home as in his own country. The authority of its ruler lies over the whole of Christianity. By his own will he, as the supreme arbiter of right and wrong, can compel the obedience of strangers in their own lands, just the same as if they were denizens of Rome. Considerations of birth have no weight in the promotion of men to high office in his court. The freedom given under the government of Venice, and the conveniences of traffic, attract thither vast numbers of foreigners, but they are nevertheless like men in a stranger city; while here foreigners will be found in special offices carrying emolument and responsibility, for Rome is the home of all those connected with the Church. As many or perhaps more strangers may be seen in Venice (where the multitude of these far exceeds anything of the sort in France or Germany), but not nearly so many resident or domiciled foreigners. The common people are no longer affronted by the sight of a man dressed in French, or Spanish, or German fashion, and nearly every beggar who begged alms of me spoke my own tongue.

However, I sought in every way and used all my five natural senses to win for myself the title of Roman citizen, if only for the ancient renown and religious association clinging to the position attached to this citizenship.

4

The Sack of Rome

16

LUIGI GUICCIARDINI

The Sack of Rome

1527

Luigi Guicciardini (1478–1551), a Florentine aristocrat and diplomat who advised the ill-fated Pope Clement VII, provides a detailed political and military account of the disastrous sack of Rome from a pro-papal perspective. He shared with his younger brother Francesco, known as the father of modern history, a desire to relate the facts as he knew them. His narrative is journalistic in style, initially drafted as events transpired and based on personal observation. Other documents concerned with the sack have wider aims: either to raise issues of papal negligence, corruption, and incompetence (Document 20) or to use the disaster as an occasion for humor (Documents 17 and 19). Nonetheless, Luigi Guicciardini may strike the modern reader as far more ready to express moral judgments than we might expect in current historical writing. In recounting the events surrounding the sack of Rome, he also paints a vivid portrait of the diverse people who constituted the city.

The Roman people and resident aliens, who had taken a census of themselves a few days before that totaled about thirty-thousand combatants, considered themselves invincible, the way people usually do before they look danger in the face. More often than any other officer of Our Lord,

Luigi Guicciardini, *The Sack of Rome*, trans. and ed. James H. McGregor (New York: Italica Press, 1993), 84–85, 87–88, 92–93, 97–99, 106–16.

Signor Renzo da Ceri declared his opinion that the enemy could not last two days outside the walls because of their extreme lack of food; and that on the second day the army of the [pro-papal] League would enter Rome. This made the people feel even more secure. The datary [papal treasurer Gian Matteo Giberti], too, and Jacopo Salviati [a Florentine adviser to the pope], along with many others, were so certain of victory that not only would they not permit the pope to leave, but they also prevented the merchants from Florence and other places from putting their wives and their most valuable goods into a galleon and various other ships, which they had hired for the purpose, and sending them immediately towards Civitavecchia. Instead they had the gates of the city closed. They declared that such fears were ridiculous and unnecessary, and that this was no time to permit things that could cause panic among those who remained in the city. They also argued that it would increase the hopes and stubbornness of the enemy, if they saw people fleeing and goods being shipped out. As a result of these arguments, it seems that the majority in Rome anticipated the assault on the walls without fear. . . .

While preparations were being made inside and outside Rome, the dawn of May 6 was approaching. Almost everything was already in order in the imperial army, and a large detachment of troops was approaching that part of the city wall near Santo Spirito. Monseigneur de Bourbon, all in armor with a loose white coat worn over it, was continually to be seen riding here and there on horseback, comforting and encouraging his troops. To the Spanish and German veterans of Milan, he would say: "Now for the third time you must show that strength and ferocity that we have seen in you twice before; for the riches and the glory that you earned in those victories will be lost—as well as your lives—if your energy flags at this point." He told the Italians that it was every bit as necessary to show their valor at this point as it had been in their other campaigns. If they didn't win today, they would be better off taking their own lives than falling into the hands of the enemy. There was nowhere for them to go, he said, for those in this incomparable army stood alone against all the forces of the League. Beyond this, he offered again what he had promised them so many times before, declaring that in addition to their portion of the booty, they would become lords and rulers of their native cities and towns.

To the Lutherans who had come with Captain von Frundsberg, he recalled the great discomforts, the intolerable hunger, and the extreme lack of money that they had endured for no other purpose than to reach the walls of Rome. And if they showed the fire he knew they had in them, it was certain that in a very few hours they would be inside the city with their wives and children. Then they would be rich and secure, enjoying the incredible wealth of vicious and ridiculous prelates. And continually riding through the camp, wherever he saw a large number of armed men together, he approached to give them comfort and encourage them to go forward. Again and again he promised that he was going to be among the first to climb over those famous walls. By his readiness and courage, he tried to show the army that he thought victory was certain. As a result of his care and encouragement, the infantry and cavalry forces were in order before dawn, no less eager than ready to attack energetically. . . .

Inside the castello [Castel Sant' Angelo] a crowd of prelates, merchants, nobles, courtiers, women, and soldiers gathered at the principal entrance, mixed up and pressed together so tightly that they prevented the closing of the gate. Finally those inside dropped the portcullis, even though it slid down and was secured only with great difficulty because it had not been inspected earlier and cleaned of rust. Those without were forced to accept the fact that if they wished to save themselves, they would have to go elsewhere. There were already more than three thousand people inside the castello. A large number of important people, prelates, and other notables were among them, plus all the cardinals except for Valle, Aracoeli, Cesarini, Siena, and Enckenvoirt. Because they were leaders of the Ghibelline faction [pro-Holy Roman emperor], these cardinals thought they would be more secure in their own palaces and didn't want to be enclosed in the castello. . . .

Meanwhile the rest of the Roman people, as well as the merchants, prelates, courtiers, and foreigners all ran back and forth in great confusion and terror looking for some refuge. Running through the streets as if they were lost, unable to leave Rome because the gates were barred, they entered the strongest places or those they considered the safest. Some took refuge in the Colonna houses, others in those of the Spanish, Flemish, and Germans who had lived for many years in Rome, and many others in the palaces of Cardinals Enckenvoirt, Aracoeli, Siena, Cesarini, and Valle. . . .

When they realized that all the defenders had fled and that they were truly in control of the city, the Spanish troops began to capture houses (along with everyone and everything that was in them) and to take prisoners. Those that they came upon as they fled in confusion through the streets, they also took captive rather than killing them. The Germans, however, were obeying the articles of war and cutting to pieces anyone they came upon (an act that is very necessary in the first hours of a victory). When they saw how the Spanish were acting, the Germans began to fear betrayal. They were quickly persuaded, however, by the Spanish captains that since the city was abandoned by its defenders, and that great riches must have been hidden in it, it would be a grave mistake not to keep alive anyone who might be able to show them where treasures were hidden or give them the names of people outside Rome who would pay their ransoms.

So then the lancers also began to take captive whomever they encountered and to break into the most beautiful houses they saw. And in a short time nearly everyone was taken prisoner, for they had no respect for the sacred places where (as always in such crises) many women, children, and frightened men had taken refuge. Divine things were treated no differently by them than profane ones. And rushing continually here and there like Furies from hell, they searched every sacred place and, with terrible violence, broke into any building they chose. Wherever they encountered resistance, they fought with ferocity; and if they could not overcome the defenders, they set the place on fire. Many priceless objects and many people who would not surrender themselves into their bestial hands were burned and consumed.

How many courtiers, how many genteel and cultivated men, how many refined prelates, how many devoted nuns, virgins, or chaste wives with their little children became the prey of these cruel foreigners! How many calixes, crosses, statues, and vessels of silver and gold were stolen from the altars, sacristies, and other holy places where they were stored. How many rare and venerable relics, covered with gold and silver, were despoiled by bloody, homicidal hands and hurled with impious derision to the earth. The heads of St. Peter, St. Paul, St. Andrew and many other saints; the wood of the Cross, the Thorns, the Holy Oil, and even consecrated Hosts were shamefully trodden underfoot in that fury.

In the street you saw nothing but thugs and rogues carrying great bundles of the richest vestments and ecclesiastical ornaments and huge sacks full of all kinds of vessels of gold and silver—testifying more to the riches and empty pomp of the Roman curia than to the humble poverty and true devotion of the Christian religion. Great numbers of captives of all sorts were to be seen, groaning and screaming, being swiftly led to makeshift prisons. In the streets there were many corpses. Many nobles lay there cut to pieces, covered with mud and their own blood, and many people only half dead lay miserably on the ground. Sometimes in that ghastly scene a child or man would be seen jumping from a window, forced to jump or jumping voluntarily to escape becoming the living prey of these monsters and finally ending their lives horribly in the street.

It did the Colonna and the Ghibellines no good to be of that faction, because the victors had no more regard for that party than for the other; nor did they treat the Spaniards, the Germans, and the Flemish who had lived a long time in Rome any better than any Italian courtier or clergyman. Those cardinals who had not taken refuge in the castello received no respect or deference; even though they had convinced themselves beforehand that they would be well treated because of their dignity, their extraordinary costumes, and the fact that they were no less wicked than the other leaders of the imperial party. Instead they were quickly made prisoners in their own palaces along with all those who had taken refuge there for their own safety. . . .

So picking up where I left off, I note that after the Spanish and Germans had rested and recuperated somewhat from the incredible fatigue they incurred while scouring the city for booty, they began with many painful and cruel tortures to interrogate their prisoners. Their aim was to discover both hidden riches and the quantity of money their prisoners were able to pay for their liberation. Because they were pitiless and without respect for rank, sex, or age (like vile beasts), those whom they tortured exposed their hiding places; and many, in order to escape from present torture, agreed to ransoms so large that afterwards it was impossible for them to pay. Those who resisted and stubbornly refused to give the enemy the designated sum endured intolerable sufferings worse even than the unbearable fear of certain death. Indeed, they experienced every conceivable form of suffering up to the very point of death. And even though those who were being tortured cried out continually for death, the cruel and greedy Spaniards skillfully kept them alive, and there is no doubt that they would have experienced much less pain at the separation of their souls from their bodies. . . .

When in the midst of such horror these savages wanted to amuse themselves, using similar tortures, they would force the prelates and courtiers to confess to their infamous and criminal habits. The obscenity and filth of their actions not only amazed and stupefied the foreigners, but forced them to admit that they would never have imagined that the human intellect could conceive of such shameful and bestial things, let alone do them. For the sake of ridicule and punishment, they carried Cardinal Aracoeli one day on a bier through every street in Rome as if he were dead, continually chanting his eulogy. They finally carried his "body" to a church where with great pleasure about half of his unusual (out of reverence, I will avoid saying "criminal") habits were detailed in a funeral oration, along with those of other cardinals and prelates. Returning afterwards to his palace, they refreshed themselves in his presence with the finest wines voraciously drunk from consecrated chalices of gold. Later the same cardinal was seen in various parts of Rome as a prisoner, on some Spaniard's back, in order to force him more quickly to come up with his ransom. . . .

A priest was shamelessly and cruelly killed because he refused to administer the most holy sacrament to a mule in clerical vestments. I will not describe what happened to the noble and beautiful young matrons, to virgins and nuns, in order not to shame anyone. The majority were ransomed, and anyone can easily imagine for himself what must have happened when these women found themselves in the hands of such lustful people as the Spaniards. Since they devoted such energy and skill to the task of making their prisoners pay incomparable sums of money in order to escape from their hands, it is probable that they applied the same methods in order to insure the satisfaction of their hot and intemperate libidos. Many are convinced that in this scene of outrage and terror, many noble and pure virgins, rather than fall into the hands of their lustful conquerors, stabbed themselves or leapt from some high point into the Tiber. I, however, have never heard that anyone has been able to positively identify a woman of such virtue and chastity. This should not be surprising considering how corrupt Rome is at present, how full of abominable vices and entirely lacking in the virtues it possessed in Antiquity.

I know that I am about to say things that many people will have difficulty in believing. Namely that the German and Lutheran soldiers, even though they are thought to be more inhumane and more prejudiced against the Italians than the Spanish, this time showed themselves to be more benign, less greedy, and much more tractable by nature than either the Spanish or Italian troops of the emperor. Many Germans, after the first furious wave of the attack was over, did not force their prisoners to undergo extensive torture, but they were content and satisfied with the sums of money that were offered freely. And many of them were both humane and respectful towards gentlewomen (even when they were young and beautiful). They brought them food and kept them at a distance from other prisoners, where they would not be insulted or injured by others. Consequently many prisoners at any early point in their capture, offering a small amount of money in comparison to what they could actually pay, were liberated without difficulty. This liberality and easygoing nature of the Germans is not to be attributed to their inexperience or to the fact that because they were very poor, every little offer of money seemed a lot to them. But it reflects a more humane and moderate nature. Certainly no one ever heard that the Spanish in their first raids, even though they were extremely poor, ever behaved towards their prisoners with such compassion and respect. . . .

The immense riches of the Roman nobility, preserved in their families for many centuries, were destroyed in an hour. The incredible profits that had been accumulated and multiplied unjustly and dishonestly through years of usury, theft, simony, and other immoral means by courtiers and merchants fell in an instant into the hands of these barbarians. But why do I bother to recount the details of various fortunes or possessions that fell in such short time into the hands of these savage foreigners? Everybody knows that money, merchandise, and delicacies from all over Europe and much of the rest of the world came pouring into that city every hour to satisfy the insatiable appetites and the illicit desires of its many licentious prelates and courtiers. Because they had never feared that they might lose their possessions, the Romans were surprised, sacked, and slaughtered with incredible ease and enormous profit. . . .

By the same token, no one would now recognize the cardinals, patriarchs, archbishops, bishops, protonotaries, generals, provincials, guardians, abbots, vicars, and all the rest of the ridiculous and infinite tribe of modern religious title-holders, who dishonor and burden the Christian religion. Now many of these men wore torn and disgraceful habits, others were without shoes. Some in torn and bloody shirts had cuts and bruises all over their bodies from the indiscriminate whippings and beatings they had received. Some had thick and greasy beards. Some had their faces branded; and some were missing teeth; others were without noses or ears. Some were castrated and so depressed and terrified that they failed to show in any way the vain and effeminate delicacy and lasciviousness that they had put on with such excessive energy for so many years in their earlier, happy days.

Not a few of these men could be seen taking care of the horses. Others turned the roasting spits and scrubbed the pots as scullery boys. Others carried wood, bedding straw, and water to their enemies and performed an infinity of other base services, as no doubt the majority of them had done before they acquired, through the exercise of wicked and shameful vices, the ranks they had never earned.

The sumptuous palaces of the cardinals, the proud palaces of the pope, the holy churches of Peter and Paul, the private chapel of His Holiness [known as] the Sancta Sanctorum, and the other holy places, once full of plenary indulgences and venerable relics, now became the brothels of German and Spanish whores. And in place of the false ceremonies and lavish music, now you could hear the horses cough and neigh, and men cursing God and all the saints. They committed shameful acts on the altars and in the most sanctified places, in contempt of contemporary religion. Many sacred pictures and sculptures that had once been worshipped with vain ceremonies were burned and broken by iron and fire. Crucifixes were shattered by shots from arquebuses and lay on the ground; the relics and calvaries of saints lay among the dung of men and animals.

All the sacraments of the modern Church were scorned and vilified as if the city had been captured by Turks or Moors or some other barbarous and infidel enemy. There was no sin or villainy that these mad and impious Lutherans did not commit. When they saw the Germans dishonoring the churches and the most holy relics, the Spanish took this very badly; they began to curse the Germans, and they came very close to violence on this score. But in the end this disagreement was settled, and the situation quieted down; the Germans stopped destroying holy images and gave their full attention to tormenting their prisoners and revisiting the same houses. And the booty continually grew, since they always found something that had been hidden before but newly revealed by their prisoners.

I will not write of the anguish and confusion that those in Castel Sant' Angelo are enduring. With the pope, there are thirteen cardinals, innumerable prelates, lords, noblewomen, merchants, couriers and soldiers, all in terror and despairing of their safety. Since they are completely surrounded and very carefully watched by their enemies, I have little knowledge of what is going on inside. We can imagine, though (since they know that they cannot escape) that they spend their time blaming Jacopo Salviati, the datary, Signor Renzo, Cardinal Armellini, and perhaps the pontiff himself, in sharp and venomous words for their obvious and multiple mistakes. No doubt it is pointless, but many blame their own past patience; and there are many among them who could not be blamed if they took cruel and fatal vengeance on these men, before the eyes of the Holy Father.

One can easily imagine the anguish and torment of the pope, constantly seeing and hearing such a scourge of punishment raised against himself and against Rome. Like the rest of those under siege, he is suffering in fear that he will soon fall into the hands of cruel enemies, obviously thirsting for his blood. And though he enjoyed great honors and sweet pleasures in the past, now he is paying for them with humiliation and pitiful distress. If he ever considered himself a wise and glorious prince, now he must acknowledge himself to be the most unfortunate and the most abject pontiff who ever lived. And since it is his fault that the Church, Rome, and Italy all find themselves in such extreme danger, we can easily imagine that he often looks toward the sky with tears in his eyes and with the bitterest and deepest sighs demands:

> "Wherefore, then, hast thou brought me forth out of the womb? Oh, that I had died, and no eye had seen me!" [Job. 10:18]

THE END OF THE HISTORY OF THE SACK OF ROME

17

FRANCISCO DELICADO

La Lozana Andaluza

1528

The cliché that fiction may be truer than fact certainly applies to La Lozana Andaluza, *a work that draws directly from the author's experiences on the streets of Rome. This long-ignored masterpiece—now hailed as one of Europe's earliest picaresque novels—appeared a century before the Spanish genre featuring roguish heroes and heroines came fully to the foreground. The story brings to life in vivid detail the wily ways of its heroine Lozana, an immigrant from Spain who seeks to make her way in the economy and society of lower-class Rome. She hustles, procures, and tricks, gliding along with assorted pimps, prostitutes, and thieves among Neapolitans, fellow Spaniards, and especially Jews—all ready to start each new day with boundless optimism, a quick smile, and an opportunistic eye for the next sucker to pass along the street. By her side is the character Rampin, initially her guide and later her husband. Historians in recent decades have come to appreciate the importance of fiction in understanding the values and workings of a society. Lozana's story fully mirrors the experiences of non-elite women in Renaissance Rome.*

Very little is known about the novel's author, Francisco Delicado (ca. 1480–ca. 1535). Internal evidence suggests that he was

Francisco Delicado, *La Lozana Andaluza,* trans. Bruno M. Damiani (Potomac, Md.: Scripta Humanistica, 1987), 16–18, 37–41, 59–66, 138, 290–91.

*a converso, or converted Jew, who had intimate knowledge of the
local street scene because that is where he grew up. At some point,
he became a priest, and he also spent years as a patient at Rome's
San Giacomo hospital, suffering from venereal disease.* La Lozana
Andalusa *relies on a dialogue format commonly used in Renaissance literary texts (see Documents 20 and 21). It is divided into
sixty-six short sketches. The excerpt here begins as Lozana, having
suffered the early loss of her parents and the abduction of her
children by her dead husband's in-laws, tries to make a new life for
herself on the streets of Rome.*

Sketch 5

HOW LOZANA EARNED HER LIVING MAKING USE OF CHEEK INSTEAD OF WIT.

AUTHOR: No sooner had Mistress Lozana arrived in the Eternal City than
the thought suddenly occurred to her: "I know a great deal; if I don't
further my cause by letting everyone know of my wisdom, it will all
go for nothing." And since she was beautiful and talkative, and said
things at the right time with charm and grace, she could easily fool
all who heard her. Then too, she was a past master at the art of conversation who had always mingled with fine people of great means,
and aware that wealth, banquets, and expense always brought her
success, she muttered to herself: "If I lack these things I'm as good as
dead, for as the saying goes, food is the music of love." And since she
had great insight and diabolical cunning, just by looking at a man she
could tell how much he was worth, how much he had, how much he
could provide her, and how much she could steal from him. She also
watched others who were in the city at that time and learned from
them what she must do to remain free and under no one's sway, as
we shall soon recount. . . .

Once she had made common knowledge of her Spanish birth, she
quickly found someone who took a liking to her and gave her a room
in the company of four worthy Spanish women. But the next day she
quarreled with them over a pitcher and kicked all four of them down
the stairs. So out she went and began to ply her trade throughout Pozo
Blanco, procuring from Castilian seamstresses whatever lodging or
companionship she could. At that time there was in Pozo Blanco a
woman from Naples who had a son and two daughters. They made
their living concocting facial preparations with powders, rouges, and
creams, plucking eyebrows and beautifying betrothed women, while

they prepared treatments of rock candy lotions from the jujube tree and astringents for female parts. They performed their trade flawlessly, and what they didn't know, some Jewish women, who practiced the same profession, taught them. Outstanding among these was Mira from Murcia, not to mention Engracia, Perla, Jamila, Rosa, Cufa, Cintia, and Alfarutia. There was also a lady called the Jew from Borgo who plied her trade well and talked a blue streak. But it should be said that Lozana knew the business better than any of them and practiced it with more skill, and we can honestly report that no one in our time has ever done better at this profession, nor earned a better return than Lozana did, as we shall disclose later on. Among them she was like Avicenna [famed Arab physician] among the physicians: the accomplishments of someone from such a clever race of people will surprise no one.

Sketch 12

LOZANA: My son, do me this favor. Wherever we go, tell me about everything and what the names of the streets are.

RAMPIN: This is the mint where money is made. And here is the way to the Campo de Flor and the Colosseum. Over there is the bridge. And these gentlemen are moneychangers.

LOZANA: You can forget about them, for I've always handled my money well.

RAMPIN: Come over here and take a look. Here the finest products from Rome and her outskirts are bought and sold.

LOZANA: What a place! Here, take this ducat and buy whatever your heart desires. And unless my eyes deceive me, this is a garden.

RAMPIN: You'll see more of it before long.

LOZANA: You don't mean it! Now why don't you buy those three partridges over there so we can dine?

RAMPIN: These little ones? They certainly are small. The other day I had one like that at the home of a courtesan. My mother had gone there to pluck the jade's eyebrows, and I carried the preparations.

LOZANA: Where does she live?

RAMPIN: Up ahead on the street we are following.

LOZANA: Well, I want to see all of this for myself.

RAMPIN: I'll be glad to show you.

LOZANA: I want you to be my boy, and you'll sleep with me. But we'll have no lovemaking you understand; why, that fuzz on your face proves that you're still a child.

RAMPIN: If you give me a chance, I won't be just a child anymore.

LOZANA: You're quite the one, aren't you? Now go buy a few cents worth of those turnovers and find us a place to sleep.

RAMPIN: We can spend the night at the house of one of my aunts.

LOZANA: What about your mother's place?

RAMPIN: They can burn her for all I care!

LOZANA: We'll take an artichoke along.

RAMPIN: But they're all so big.

LOZANA: What difference does that make? Hang the expenses. As the saying goes, "Feast or famine."

RAMPIN: Down this street are courtesans as thick as bees in a beehive.

LOZANA: How can we tell them from the others?

RAMPIN: You'll see them behind their lattices. This part of the city is called the Street of the Bear. On down the street, you'll see many more.

LOZANA: Who's that over there? The Bishop of Cordova?

RAMPIN: No, it's not, but I wish my father lived half as well as he does. That's one of those outlandish bishops from Asia Minor.

LOZANA: Count on those Mamelukes [elite Muslim Egyptian soldiers] to live in style!

RAMPIN: Here cardinals live in the way Mamelukes do.

LOZANA: And are worshipped and glorified to boot.

RAMPIN: So are the Mamelukes.

LOZANA: Cardinals really are an arrogant breed.

RAMPIN: "Misery loves company." Look up there and see God's handiwork in Lady Clarina. There she is! That's a woman of breeding for you!

LOZANA: My friend, "there is beauty in a whore, and strength in a stallion."

RAMPIN: Now look at the other one.

LOZANA: A dish fit for a king! No wonder she's such a success. And that is why they say, "Who made you a lady of easy virtue? Why, the wines and the desserts."

RAMPIN: She's a favorite of the prelate. And over here dwells the gallant Portuguese lady.

LOZANA: What is she, the friend to some man from Genoa?

RAMPIN: That lady has more friends than my grandfather has ancestors.

LOZANA: Who is that streetwalker hidden under her huge hat? The one swinging her rear and followed by two young girls?

RAMPIN: Who is she? Why some common tart from hereabouts. And just look, will you, at the fuss those women are causing over there. They look like a swarm of queen bees with their drones bringing up the rear! This is when they come out on the street wearing their disguises.

LOZANA: What are they doing?

RAMPIN: Why to get indulgences.

LOZANA: Really? Indulgences for whores? What good will that do them?

RAMPIN: Right now they are contracting business for the night.

LOZANA: Now what in the world is that?

RAMPIN: Those women are being taken away by the law.

LOZANA: Now don't run after them. We can't get involved with the likes of that!

RAMPIN: Don't worry, we won't. I'll be right back. (Exits).

LOZANA: Just look at that cock of the walk go! He certainly knows the ladies!

(To Rampin) What was it, my boy?

RAMPIN: Not a great deal. They all have to pay a fine. To keep the matter quiet, some have parted with their rings and others their necklaces. Later on each of them will be sentenced according to how much she paid. One thing is certain: they all must pay a ducat each year to the captain of the Torre Savella.

LOZANA: All of them?

RAMPIN: Except for the married ones.

LOZANA: It's wrong that only the ones working in brothels have to pay.

RAMPIN: That's why most of the city is a brothel and why they call it "Rome, the Harlot."

LOZANA: And who are those women, Moors?

RAMPIN: No, of course not. They're Romans!

LOZANA: Then why are they wearing Moorish cloaks?

RAMPIN: Wrong again! Those are Roman cloaks made of striped cloth.

LOZANA: And you mean to tell me that they dress like that all over Italy?

RAMPIN: They have ever since the days of Rodriguillo the Spaniard.

LOZANA: I'd like to know more about that.

RAMPIN: All I know is what I've heard. I can show you a bronze statue of Rodriguillo the Spaniard on the Campidolio. He's taking a thorn out of his foot and he's as naked as a jay bird.

LOZANA: Now there's a wonderful thing to know about and to see! In those days we were lucky to find two Spaniards in all of Rome. Now there are thousands. But the time will come when there won't be any at all, and when everyone will say "wretched Rome" as they say "wretched Spain" today.

RAMPIN: Do you see that steam bath, where those Roman ladies are coming out?

LOZANA: Good Lord; let's go over there ourselves! . . .

Sketch 15

HOW LOZANA AND RAMPIN WANDERED THROUGHOUT ROME LOOKING AT THE WONDERS, UNTIL THEY CAME TO THE QUARTER RESERVED FOR THE JEWS, WHERE THEY SET UP HOUSEKEEPING.

LOZANA: Which way should we go?

RAMPIN: This way, through the Plaza Redonda, where you'll see the Pantheon, the tomb of Lucretia, the obelisk containing the ashes of Romulus and Remus, the marvelous column of Marcus Aurelius, and the building constructed to Severus. After that you will take your ease at the home of a good friend of mine of long standing.

LOZANA: I tell you though, Rampin, that pure and simple uncle of yours is nothing more than an old goat. Your aunt likes me well, however, and I shall teach her much of what I know of the art.

RAMPIN: Take care, Mistress Lozana! Don't share what you know with others. Save it yourself for a day of need. Say your husband fails to appear; you'll make a tidy living yourself; especially so because I'll tell the ladies that your knowledge is greater than my mother's. And, if you wish me to stay at your side, I'll sell your wares and hawk them as special secrets from the Levante.

LOZANA: Well, so be it then, for I wish the same, that you stay with me. I have no husband, nor am I tormented by love. From this day forth, I'll keep fine clothes on your back, and you'll live as well as one of the King's own men. You'll not be worked to weariness, but you must play deaf and dumb to what I do. I command you to hold your tongue, even when I scold you severely and treat you like my serving boy. If you do, you'll always have the best part. What I earn you will look after. And you'll soon see that we'll have need of no one else. . . .

RAMPIN: It shall be as you say, and I'll fetch it [supplies for medicinal creams] for you myself. But before that let us speak with Trigo, the Jewish merchant, who will lease you what you need and will take the obligation of the house as well.

LOZANA: What more could we ask? But are you known hereabouts?

RAMPIN: You do better to put yourself in Trigo's hands. He is crafty and will spread your fame among rich men who will hire the house and buy your food.

LOZANA: Such do I receive readily. But tell me, is that this merchant, Trigo, that I see nearby?

RAMPIN: Trigo has friends in high places and has no need to wear a red badge. While he works he dresses in silks. That merchant over there is dressed in tatters and smelly rags.

LOZANA: What square is this?

RAMPIN: It's called Navona. If you come here on Wednesdays you'll see a market like nothing you've ever seen in all your born days, so orderly and complete in every care under the sun. Look here for whatever you need and you shall find it, be it grown on earth or living in the depths of the sea. All needs are richly catered here, in abundance, like the market in Venice or any other land that traffics in goods from beyond the sea.

LOZANA: Well, this I certainly want you to show me. In Cordova, if I remember aright, market day was Thursday:

> Thursday, it was Thursday.
> On market day.
> That Hernando did invite
> The Commanders.

Oh, if only I had died when first I heard that sorry song! No. I really don't mean that either, for life is good; it is in living that we praise the Lord. Now who are those men who stared at me? The world is their oyster, while dismal is the lot of those who must go on foot and bathed only in sweat. See how poorly they treat their mules, their backs almost broken by the packs they carry, and their women trailing along behind.

RAMPIN: The women are but common tarts, but the men must be great lords. So is it said, "Observe Rome, the glory of men of power, a paradise for whores, a purgatory for the young, a fraud for the poor, a drudgery for the beast of burden, a market place for swindlers and a hell for all."

LOZANA: What's that man preaching over there? Let's go over and see.

RAMPIN: He's preaching about the loss and destruction of Rome in 1527, but he's making a joke out of it. Here is Campo de Flor, the very center of the city. Those you see are the charlatans, the quack dentists, the butcher surgeons who cheat the country bumpkins and all newcomers, whom they call the needy ones.

LOZANA: And how do they cheat them?

RAMPIN: Do you see that root that he has in his hand? He's saying that it cures toothaches and that he'll sell it for a *bayoque*, worth about four *cuatrines*. He'll make more than a hundred of them, if he can find enough fools to buy those roots of his and think of all the *cuatrines* he'll have. Watch that bloated pig waving his piece of paper about. He's saying that his powders will purge away worms, and they might as well be earthworms for all the good they will do. Just look how fast he's talking, for up his sleeve he has other trinkets, worth even less than a *cuatrine*. He'll tell them all a thousand lies and they'll end up emptyhanded. Let's get out of here! As the saying goes, "one lunatic can make a hundred more."

LOZANA: Upon my soul, they aren't mad! I ask you, is there anyone more clever than the man who can pick another's pocket without getting caught? But what in the world have we here? Why are all those young men scurrying about that gentleman?

RAMPIN: They're servants looking for masters.

LOZANA: And they come here?

RAMPIN: Yes, ma'am, they do. Do you see those two young men walking arm in arm with that fine gentleman they are all trying to impress? Their service with him will be a rocky year at best, and then he'll search for others.

LOZANA: How do you come to know this, Rampin? That grandmother of all washerwomen told me yesterday that new workers are hired in this province every day.

RAMPIN: What does that ancient bawd know about it? When servants are honest and care for their masters' clothing, they have no need to leave in a day's time, but if they wish to own the finery their masters have worked to buy, they'll be shown the door soon enough. Just think how many servants and maids slander the house they work for, speak evil of their employers, steal more than they earn, and hide a chest in the bushes to hold their ill-gotten gain. If the maids can't have their young men visit at night, they go out themselves. But the masters have so much need of them that they tolerate it, and when they do find new servants, thinking they are better, they get good service for only a month or so. There is nothing worse in these parts than finding new help, but the masters could care less, for if a maid quits another begs for employment. Hence the servants never manage to live well and their masters never make them their heirs, as they do in other places. Just imagine! I have served two masters the last three months. The last one was a squire. It was he who gave me these silk slippers. He kept a whore and we used to eat food that we ordered from the tavern. She was a real glutton, but he got the idea I had eaten a few wild pears sitting on the table and dismissed me. And since I had no contract with him, but was hired at his pleasure, all I had for my trouble was this French footwear. I had hoped that one day he might let me have a few of the fine things he didn't need.

LOZANA: Is that the truth you tell me? Then you don't know what they say, do you? "The fool feeds on hope." Your master was a simpleton, and you, my fine friend, were a fool.

Sketch 16

HOW THEY ENTERED THE JEWISH QUARTER OF THE CITY, AND HOW TRIGO WENT ABOUT SETTING UP LOZANA IN HOUSEKEEPING.

LOZANA: My nose tells me there's good cooking around. They must be having a feast. My goodness, it smells like roast pig!

RAMPIN: Can't you see that only Jews live here? It's Saturday morning, and they're making their fricassee. Look at those braziers and the cooking vessels hanging above them.

LOZANA: Yes, of course! The Jews are past masters at using charcoal. There is nothing better anywhere than a meal cooked over a charcoal fire in an earthen pot. But tell me the name of that building over there, where so many persons are gathering?

RAMPIN: Let's go over there and you'll see. This synagogue is for Catalan men, and the one further along is for their women. The synagogue down there is for the Germans, and the neighboring one is for the French. This one is for the Romans and Italians, the worst Jews of all because they act like Gentiles and don't even remember their own laws. Our Spaniards know more than any of the others, for they count many learned and rich men among them and are very wise. Just look at their gathering over there. What do you think of them? That synagogue takes the cake. Those two men are close friends of ours, and I know their wives, for they go throughout Rome teaching prayers to those who are about to be wed and ways of fasting to the young girls to ensure a child the first year. . . .

Sketch 31

LOZANA: I want to live by my own labor. I have never bothered married women or virgins; I have never sold young girls or carried messages to anyone I wasn't sure was a whore, or become involved with married men to bring down the wrath of their wives upon my head. I only want to live by my profession. Let me tell you: when first I came to Rome, I tried to learn about all the possible ways I could earn my daily bread. I didn't know then what I know now, that if I took up with courtesans, I would soon rub elbows with the women of Rome, but as the saying goes, "something is better than nothing." . . .

[Lozana has many other adventures in Rome and marries Rampin; when the sack of Rome destroys her means of livelihood, she goes with him to live on the island of Lipari, off the coast of Sicily. The text closes with Lozana's letter to all women who have decided to come to see Campo dei Fiori in the heart of Rome.]

Friends and sisters in love: Because I desire the same thing you do and because I have paused to consider the matter carefully for love of you, and because I fear for you, I thought of warning you about what happened in Rome when fourteen thousand Teutonic barbarians; seven thousand Spaniards without weapons, without shoes, hungry and thirsty; fifteen hundred Italians; two thousand Neapolitan soldiers attached to the King, all of these infantrymen; six hundred armed men, thirty five mounted standard bearers; plus the quartermasters, for almost all of them are given to pillaging, invaded, punished, tormented and sacked us. For if Rome is not completely destroyed, it is because of the devoted female sex and the charity and refuge that it currently provided for these pilgrims. Everything has been forbidden. . . . [I]t is better for you not to come, because there is no rhyme or reason to it. If you come to see abbots, they are all emptying their testicles; if to see merchants, they have become poor; if to see famous gentlemen, they are busy seeking the peace they lost and cannot find; if to see Roman men, they are rebuilding and planting their vineyards; if to see courtiers, they are so poor that they cannot even get bread. If you come to triumph, do not come because triumph belongs to the past; if for charity, you will find it exaggerated here so much that its excesses are smeared on the wall. Therefore, be calm, for, without a doubt for many years, you will be able to spin large, long veils. Be assured that, if Lozana were able to celebrate the past or to speak about the present without fear, she would not absent herself from you or from Rome, especially since it is everyone's homeland and because "Roma" written backwards spells "amor."

18

BENVENUTO CELLINI

The Autobiography of Benvenuto Cellini
1558–1563

The sculptor Benvenuto Cellini (1500–1571) turned late in life to writing his autobiography and filled it with insights not only about himself and his healthy ego but also about the Roman world in which he thrived. His native Florence, which he defends with his sword as this document opens, occasionally served him as a retreat, but always he returned to the money, the hustle, the vibrancy, and the sheer lunacy of Rome's street life. He was there in the daytime to defend his adopted city against its invaders in the 1527 sack. And he was certainly there many nights, in and around Piazza Navona, seeking the allurements of sex for sale and brandishing his sword in alcohol-fueled street brawls.

Since I am writing my life, I must from time to time diverge from my profession in order to describe with brevity, if not in detail, some incidents which have no bearing on my career as artist. On the morning of Saint John's Day I happened to be dining with several men of our nation [Florence], painters, sculptors, goldsmiths, amongst the most notable of whom was Rosso and Gianfrancesco, the pupil of Raffaello. I had invited them without restraint or ceremony to the place of our meeting, and they were all laughing and joking, as is natural when a crowd of men come together to make merry on so great a festival. It chanced that a light-brained swaggering young fellow passed by; he was a soldier of Rienzo da Ceri, who, when he heard the noise that we were making, gave vent to a string of opprobrious sarcasms upon the folk of Florence. I, who was the host of those great artists and men of worth, taking the insult to myself, slipped out quietly without being observed, and went up to him. I ought to say that he had a punk of his there, and was going on with his stupid ribaldries to amuse her. When I met him, I asked if he was the rash fellow who was speaking evil of the Florentines.

John Addington Symonds, ed., *The Autobiography of Benvenuto Cellini* (Garden City, N.Y.: Garden City Publishing Co., 1927), 43–50, 98–99, 101–2, 122–24, 132.

He answered at once: "I am that man." On this I raised my hand, struck him in the face, and said: "And I am *this* man." Then we each of us drew our swords with spirit; but the fray had hardly begun when a crowd of persons intervened, who rather took my part than not, hearing and seeing that I was in the right.

On the following day a challenge to fight with him was brought me, which I accepted very gladly, saying that I expected to complete this job far quicker than those of the other art I practiced. So I went at once to confer with a fine old man called Bevilacqua, who was reputed to have been the first sword of Italy, because he had fought more than twenty serious duels and had always come off with honor. This excellent man was a great friend of mine; he knew me as an artist and had also been concerned as intermediary in certain ugly quarrels between me and others. Accordingly, when he had learned my business, he answered with a smile: "My Benvenuto, if you had an affair with Mars, I am sure you would come out with honor, because through all the years that I have known you, I have never seen you wrongfully take up a quarrel." So he consented to be my second, and we repaired with sword in hand to the appointed place; but no blood was shed, for my opponent made the matter up, and I came with much credit out of the affair. I will not add further particulars; for though they would be very interesting in their own way, I wish to keep both space and words for my art, which has been my chief inducement to write as I am doing, and about which I shall have only too much to say. . . .

At that time [spring 1523], while I was still a young man of about twenty-three, there raged a plague of such extraordinary violence that many thousands died of it every day in Rome. Somewhat terrified at this calamity, I began to take certain amusements, as my mind suggested, and for a reason which I will presently relate. I had formed a habit of going on feast-days to the ancient buildings, and copying parts of them in wax or with the pencil; and since these buildings are all ruins, and the ruins house innumerable pigeons, it came into my head to use my gun against these birds. So then, avoiding all commerce with people, in my terror of the plague, I used to put a fowling-piece on my boy Pagolino's shoulder, and he and I went out alone into the ruins; and oftentimes we came home laden with a cargo of the fattest pigeons. . . .

As I have said above, the plague had broken out in Rome; but though I must return a little way upon my steps, I shall not therefore abandon the main path of my history. There arrived in Rome a surgeon of the highest renown, who was called Maestro Giacomo da Carpi. This able man, in the course of his other practice, undertook the most desperate cases of the so-called French disease [syphilis]. In Rome this kind of illness is very partial to the priests, and especially to the richest of them. When, therefore, Maestro Giacomo had made his talents known, he professed to work miracles in the treatment of such cases by means of certain fumigations; but he only undertook a cure after stipulating for his fees, which he reckoned not by tens, but by hundreds of crowns. . . .

The plague went dragging on for many months, but I had as yet managed to keep it at bay; for though several of my comrades were dead, I survived in health and freedom. Now it chanced one evening that an intimate comrade of mine brought home to supper a Bolognese prostitute named Faustina. She was a very fine woman, but about thirty years of age; and she had with her a little serving-girl of thirteen or fourteen. Faustina belonging to my friend, I would not have touched her for all the gold in the world; and though she declared she was madly in love with me, I remained steadfast in my loyalty. But after they had gone to bed, I stole away the little serving-girl, who was quite a fresh maid, and woe to her if her mistress had known of it! The result was that I enjoyed a very pleasant night, far more to my satisfaction than if I had passed it with Faustina. I rose upon the hour of breaking fast, and felt tired, for I had travelled many miles that night, and was wanting to take food, when a crushing headache seized me; several boils appeared on my left arm, together with a carbuncle which showed itself just beyond the palm of the left hand where it joins the wrist. Everybody in the house was in a panic; my friend, the cow and the calf, all fled. Left alone there with my poor little prentice, who refused to abandon me, I felt stifled at the heart, and made up my mind for certain I was a dead man.

Just then the father of the lad went by, who was physician to the Cardinal Iacoacci, and lived as member of that prelate's household. The boy called out: "Come, father, and see Benvenuto; he is in bed with some trifling indisposition." Without thinking what my complaint might be, the doctor came up at once, and when he had felt my pulse, he saw and felt what was very contrary to his own wishes. Turning round to his son, he cried: "O traitor of a child, you've ruined me; how can I venture now into the Cardinal's presence?" His son made answer: "Why, father, this man my master is worth far more than all the cardinals in Rome." Then the doctor turned to me and said: "Since I am here, I will consent to treat you. But of one thing only I warn you, that if you have enjoyed a woman, you are doomed." To this I replied: "I did so this very night." He answered: "With whom, and to what extent?" I said: "Last night, and with a girl in her earliest maturity." Upon this, perceiving that he had spoken foolishly, he made haste to add: "Well, considering the sores are so new, and have not yet begun to stink, and that the remedies will be taken in time, you need not be too much afraid, for I have good hopes of curing you." . . .

[Cellini served briefly in the defense of Castel Sant' Angelo during the sack of Rome but then decided to return to Florence. Eventually he accepted Pope Clement VII's plea that he return to work in Rome.]

I kept a shaggy dog, very big and handsome, which Duke Alessandro gave me; the beast was capital as a retriever, since he brought me every sort of birds and game I shot, but he also served most admirably for a watchdog. It happened, as was natural at the age of twenty-nine, that I had taken into my service a girl of great beauty and grace, whom I used as a model in my art, and who was also complaisant of her personal favors to me. Such being the case, I occupied an apartment far away from my workmen's rooms, as well as from the shop; and this communicated by a little dark passage with the maid's bedroom. I used frequently to pass the night with her; and though I sleep as lightly as ever yet did man upon this earth, yet, after indulgence in sexual pleasure, my slumber is sometimes very deep and heavy.

So it chanced one night: for I must say that a thief, under the pretext of being a goldsmith, had spied on me, and cast his eyes upon the precious stones, and made a plan to steal them. Well, then, this fellow broke into the shop, where he found a quantity of little things in gold and silver. He was engaged in bursting open certain boxes to get at the jewels he had noticed, when my dog jumped upon him, and put him to much trouble to defend himself with his sword. The dog, unable to grapple with an armed man, ran several times through the house, and rushed into the rooms of the journeymen, which had been left open because of the great heat. When he found they paid no heed to his loud barking, he dragged their bed-clothes off; and when they still heard nothing, he pulled first one and then another by the arm till he roused them, and, barking furiously, ran before to show them where he wanted them to go. At last it became clear that they refused to follow; for the traitors, cross at being disturbed, threw stones and sticks at him; and this they could well do, for I had ordered them to keep all night a lamp alight there; and in the end they shut their rooms tight; so the dog, abandoning all hope of aid from such rascals, set out alone again on his adventure. He ran down, and not finding the thief in the shop, flew after him. When he got at him, he tore the cape off his back. It would have gone hard with the fellow had he not called for help to certain tailors, praying them for God's sake to save him from a mad dog; and they, believing what he said, jumped out and drove the dog off with much trouble.

After sunrise my workmen went into the shop, and saw that it had been broken open and all the boxes smashed. They began to scream at the top of their voices: "Ah, woe is me! Ah, woe is me!" The clamor woke me, and I rushed out in a panic. Appearing thus before them, they cried out: "Alas to us! for we have been robbed by someone, who has broken and borne everything away!" These words wrought so forcibly upon my mind that I dared not go to my big chest and look if it still held the jewels of the Pope. So intense was the anxiety, that I seemed to lose my eyesight, and told them they themselves must unlock the chest, and see how many of the Pope's gems were missing. The fellows were all of them in their shirts; and when, on opening the chest, they saw the precious stones and my work with them, they took heart of joy and shouted: "There is no harm done; your piece and all the stones are here; but the thief has left us naked to the shirt, because last night, by reason of the burning heat, we took our clothes off in the shop and left them here." Recovering my senses, I thanked God, and said: "Go and get yourselves new suits of clothes; I will pay when I hear at leisure how the whole thing happened." . . .

On that very day, as I was passing through the Piazza Navona, and had my fine retriever with me, just when we came opposite the gate of the Bargello, my dog flew barking loudly inside the door upon a youth, who had been arrested at the suit of a man called Donnino (a goldsmith from Parma, and a former pupil of Caradosso), on the charge of having robbed him. The dog strove so violently to tear the fellow to pieces, that the constables were moved to pity. It so happened that he was pleading his own cause with boldness, and Donnino had not evidence enough to support the accusation; and what was more, one of the corporals of the guard, a Genoese, was a friend of the young man's father. The upshot was that, what with the dog and with those other circumstances, they were on the point of releasing their prisoner. When I came up, the dog had lost all fear of sword or staves, and was flying once more at the young man; so they told me if I did not call the brute off they would kill him. I held him back as well as I was able; but just then the fellow, in the act of readjusting his cape, let fall some paper packets from the hood, which Donnino recognized as his property. I too recognized a little ring; whereupon I called out: "This is the thief who broke into my shop and robbed it; and therefore my dog knows him;" then I loosed the dog, who flew again upon the robber. . . .

[Another street fight, and the pope intervenes.] By this time a crowd had gathered round to hear the quarrel. Provoked by his ugly words, I stooped and took up a lump of mud—for it had rained—and hurled it with a quick and unpremeditated movement at his face. He ducked his head, so that the mud hit him in the middle of the skull. There was a stone in it with several sharp angles, one of which striking him, he fell stunned like a dead man: whereupon all the bystanders, seeing the great quantity of blood, judged that he was really dead.

While he was still lying on the ground, and people were preparing to carry him away, Pompeo the jeweler passed by. The Pope had sent for him to give orders about some jewels. Seeing the fellow in such a miserable plight, he asked who had struck him; on which they told him: "Benvenuto did it, but the stupid creature brought it down upon himself." No sooner had Pompeo reached the Pope than he began to speak: "Most blessed Father, Benvenuto has this very moment murdered Tobbia; I saw it with my own eyes." On this the Pope in a fury ordered the Governor, who was in the presence, to take and hang me at once in the place where the homicide had been committed, adding that he must do all he could to catch me, and not appear again before him until he had hanged me.

When I saw the unfortunate Benedetto stretched upon the ground, I thought at once of the peril I was in, considering the power of my enemies, and what might ensue from this disaster. Making off, I took refuge in the house of Messer Giovanni Gaddi, clerk of the Camera, with the intention of preparing as soon as possible to escape from Rome. He, however, advised me not to be in such a hurry, for it might turn out perhaps that the evil was not so great as I imagined; and calling Messer Annibal Caro, who lived with him, bade him go for information.

While these arrangements were being made, a Roman gentleman appeared, who belonged to the household of Cardinal de' Medici, who had been sent by him. Taking Messer Giovanni and me apart, he told us that the Cardinal had reported to him what the Pope said, and that there was no way of helping me out of the scrape; it would be best for me to shun the first fury of the storm by flight, and not to risk myself in any house in Rome. Upon this gentleman's departure, Messer Giovanni looked me in the face as though he were about to cry, and said: "Ah me! Ah woe is me! There is nothing I can do to aid you!" I replied: "By God's means, I shall aid myself alone; only I request you to put one of your horses at my disposal." They had already saddled a black Turkish horse, the finest and the best in Rome. I mounted with an arquebuse upon the saddle-bow, wound up in readiness to fire, if need were. When I reached Ponte Sisto, I found the whole of the Bargello's guard there, both horse and foot. So, making a virtue of necessity, I put my horse boldly to a sharp trot, and with God's grace, being somehow unperceived by them, passed freely through. Then, with all the speed I could, I took the road to Palombara, a fief of my lord Giovanbatista Savello, whence I sent the horse back to Messer Giovanni, without, however, thinking it well to inform him where I was. . . .

[And another fight.] In the meanwhile my enemies had proceeded slowly toward Chiavica, as the place was called, and had arrived at the crossing of several roads, going in different directions; but the street in which Pompeo's house stood was the one which leads straight to the Campo di Fiore. Some business or other made him enter the apothecary's shop which stood at the corner of Chiavica, and there he stayed a while transacting it. I had just been told that he had boasted of the insult which he fancied he had put upon me; but be that as it may, it was to his misfortune; for precisely when I came up to the corner, he was leaving the shop and his bravi had opened their ranks and received him in their midst. I drew a little dagger with a sharpened edge, and breaking the line of his defenders, laid my hands upon his breast so quickly and coolly, that none of them were able to prevent me. Then I aimed to strike him in the face; but fright made him turn his head round; and I stabbed him just beneath the ear. I only gave two blows, for he fell stone dead at the second. I had not meant to kill him; but as the saying goes, knocks are not dealt by measure. With my left hand I plucked back the dagger, and with my right hand drew my sword to defend my life. However, all those bravi ran up to the corpse and took no action against me; so I went back alone through Strada Giulia, considering how best to put myself in safety.

I had walked about three hundred paces, when Piloto the goldsmith, my very good friend, came up and said: "Brother, now that the mischief's done, we must see to saving you." I replied: "Let us go to Albertaccio del Bene's house; it is only a few minutes since I told him I should soon have need of him." When we arrived there, Albertaccio and I embraced with measureless affection; and soon the whole flower of the young men of the Banchi, of all nations except the Milanese, came crowding in; and each and all made proffer of their own life to save mine.

19

PIETRO ARETINO

Aretino's Dialogues

1536

The fictional work known as the Ragionamenti *(Aretino's Dialogues in the English version) was not meant to be read by schoolchildren during the Renaissance or even today. Modern literary scholars debate intensely about whether Pietro Aretino (1492–1556) told the everyday truth about sex, albeit with crude language, or instead employed his pen to unleash an attack on the immorality of his times. Aretino's own luxurious lifestyle depended upon the noble and wealthy patrons whose behavior he satirized, which raises questions about his motivation and the reception by his audience. Whether the stories are deeply misogynous or precursors to women's control of their own bodies, including their use as an economic asset, is equally debatable. Either way, anyone who reads even a brief excerpt, such as the one below, will have good cause to assert that there is more to Renaissance literature than treatises on platonic love and ideal beauty.*

Aretino's work complicates our understanding of Renaissance Rome in fruitful ways. In this excerpt, mother Nanna has just finished explaining to her daughter Pippa why it is better for a woman to be a whore than a nun or a wife. The lesson continues with instruction on how to be a successful whore, which is possible only if Pippa understands that men are always ready to betray women. Mother Nanna's reasoning allows no space for male claims of virtue for defending their honor or that of their women on the battlefield. The setting for this tongue-in-cheek exercise in misandry (male-bashing) is the aftermath of the sack of Rome.

Raymond Rosenthal, trans. and ed., *Aretino's Dialogues* (Toronto: University of Toronto Press, 2005), 231–39. See Paula Findlen, "Humanism, Politics and Pornography in Renaissance Italy," in Lynn Hunt, *The Invention of Pornography: Obscenity and the Origins of Modernity, 1500–1800* (New York: Zone Books, 1993), 49–108, for a rich historical assessment of Aretino and his writings. Findlen writes: "To define Renaissance pornography is, in an essential sense, to define the intersections of sexuality, politics and learning—the constitutive elements of the culture itself" (54).

PIPPA: Let me tell you my dream, and then I'll listen to you.

NANNA: Tell it.

PIPPA: Will you unravel its meaning?

NANNA: I will.

PIPPA: This morning, just about dawn, I imagined I was in a high, large, beautiful room, whose walls were bedecked in green and yellow satin, and on its draperies were fastened gilt swords, embroidered velvet hats, caps with medallions, studded shields, paintings, and other noble accouterments. In one corner of the room stood a bed covered with curly brocade, and I, as abbotly as an abbot, sat on a crimson chair all studded with gold bosses like the Pope's chair. Around me roamed oxen, donkeys, sheep, big buffaloes, foxes, peacocks, owls, and blackbirds. It was futile for me to goad, beat, fleece, and flay them, tear out their hair, pluck the feathers or quills from their wings and tails, and deride them in every way, for they would not leave; on the contrary, they licked me from head to foot. Now I should very much like you to tell me the meaning of this apparition.

NANNA: I understand this dream as well as Daniel. You can consider yourself fortunate, because the oxen and donkeys which you goaded and beat are the skinflints who will cling to your tail even if they croak. The sheep and buffaloes are the poor men who will let themselves be clipped and skinned alive by your deceptions. The foxes I see as those astute fellows whom you will cudgel unmercifully after you've caught them in your traps. The tailless peacocks I take for rich and handsome youths; while the owls and blackbirds are the run of men, who will be lost just from seeing you and hearing you talk.

PIPPA: Where does that leave the other things?

NANNA: Go slowly: the bedecked room denotes your grandeur; the noble accouterments fastened to the draperies are the small thefts which you will snatch by stealth from the hand of one man or another; the Papal throne indicates the honors you will receive from everyone. Yes, indeed, you shall get the grand prize.

PIPPA: Wait, wait: the peacocks I dreamt about kept looking at their feet and did not squawk, as they usually do. What does it mean?

NANNA: You see, my prophecies are turning out to be true. This shows how wise you will become! And so those who because of their love for you are stranded on the beach of Barbary [Barbary coast of North Africa] will not lament. Now, listen to me and, while listening, tightly seal my statements in your mind; and may it be God's will that your mother's admonitions are enough to protect you from men's wiles! Alas! I say alas in honor of those poor women who get their asses scorched by bawds, amateur whoremasters, missives, promises, love, importunity, convenience, money, flattery, good looks, and the bad luck that grabs them by a hank of their hair. And don't think for a moment that all this just concerns whores or non-whores; no, these misfortunes strike at everyone, they cling to all. But since I want my conversation to be a banquet of the most thoughtful of viands, and since I never waited on diners, I don't quite know what to serve you first. And although the antipasto is meant to sharpen the appetite, I prefer when eating to start off with the best dish. So I shall open up with the most refined treachery I have in stock, just as a woman's pretty face is the first thing that people see: what man would care about her after seeing, instead of her face, the bad bargain of her body concealed by her dress? In fact, when they see the pretty face first, they assume that the rest is first-rate merchandise.

PIPPA: Your comparisons are always brand new. But go on.

NANNA: A baron living in Rome but not born there crawled through a hole, like the mice, and escaped from the sack of Rome. He was on some ship, and the savagery of the wild winds flung him and his many companions on the shore of a great city ruled by a lady whose name cannot be uttered. She was out for a stroll when she saw the poor man stretched on the sand, soaking wet, broken, deathly pale, his clothes torn and tattered, looking more like fear than today's Roman court resembles the rabble; and the worst of it was that the peasants, thinking him a Spanish grandee, were clustered around to do to him and his companions what bandits in a forest do to some unarmed wayfarer who has lost his way. But the lady, having sent them off with a nod of her head, approached and comforted him with her gracious aspect and kind manners, and then brought him to her palace. She had both the ship and its sailors put to rights with lordly lavishness. When she went to see the baron, who had completely recovered, she remained to hear his poem, speech, sermon, and preachment, in which he swore that he would forget her kindness when rivers ran uphill (oh men, you traitors, liars, and cheats!); and while he was bragging in the true Roman manner, the wretched creature, the ninny, devoured him with her eyes and, staring at his chest and shoulders, was transfixed. She overflowed with wonder at seeing the haughtiness of his face; his eyes gleaming with honor made her sigh, and his golden hair curled like engraved and lacquered metal did her in once and for all. Nor could she stop gazing delightedly at his comely figure, at the grace which that she-pig, Nature, had given him. She was lost in rapture before the divinity of that face. Cursed be both the face and the honeyed talk!

PIPPA: Why do you curse them?

NANNA: They are often cheats. Most of the time they trick us, and my witness is the baron's presence, which drove the lady I speak of stark raving mad. In less time than it takes for a woman to change her mind she had the table laid; and when the extremely royal supper was all prepared, she sat down with the baron beside her, and all his companions were there too, and the people of the place, side by side and successively, according to the hierarchical order established by Melchisedech [Genesis 14]. In the meantime a magnificence of silver dishes heaped with food was brought by a multitude of servants to the hungry men; and when the baron had satisfied his appetite, he presented the lady with gifts.

PIPPA: What did he give her?

NANNA: A mitre made of fine silk brocade which His Holiness wore on his head on Ash Wednesday; a pair of shoes embroidered with gold ribands with which his feet were shod on the day that Gian-Matteo, Pope Clement VII's datary, slobbered them with kisses; the pastoral of Pope Tow-Head, I mean Pope Linen; the ball atop the obelisk; a key torn from the hand of one of the guardians of St. Peter's stairs; a tablecloth from the palace's storehouse; and I don't know how many relics of the *santa santorum* which his prosopopoeia had, if one credited his boasting, rescued from the enemies' hands. Then a skillful rebec player appeared and, having tuned his instrument, sang some strange tales.

PIPPA: May God save you, what did he sing about?

NANNA: He sang of the hostility that heat has for cold, and cold for heat. He sang of why the days of summer are long and those of winter short. He sang of the link between lightning and thunder, thunder and the flash, the flash and the cloud, the cloud and the clear sky. He sang about where the rain stays when the weather is good, and where good weather goes when it rains. He sang of hail, hoar frost, snow, and mist. He sang, I believe, of the woman who rents out rooms, who refrains from laughter when her lodgers weep, and of another woman who refrains from weeping when they laugh; and at the end he sang about the fire which flickers in the butt-end of a glowworm, and as to whether a grasshopper chirrs with its body or its mouth.

PIPPA: Such lovely secrets!

NANNA: Indeed the lady of the manor, who listened to that singing like the dead listen to the *kyrie eleison* [Lord, have mercy], was already wildly infatuated by her guest's gab and gallantry, and as she seemed only to be alive when he was shooting a breeze, she began to ask him about the Popes and Cardinals. After this she begged him to tell her how priestly astuteness had let itself be caught in the claws of the demons of Malebolge [Dante, *The Inferno*, eighth circle]. Then the baron, wishing to obey her supplications and heaving one of those sighs which treacherously escape from the liver of a whore when she lays eyes on a stuffed purse, said: "Since Your Highness, my lady, wants me to remember things that make me hate my memory when it reminds me of them, I will tell you how the empress of the world [Rome] became the slave of the Spaniards; and besides I will tell you about all the miseries I have seen. But what Marrano [secret Jew], what German, what Jew could be so cruel as to relate these things without bursting into tears?" Then he went on: "My lady, it is time for bed, and already the stars are vanishing; but if it is your wish to know our story, even though it renew my sorrow, I will begin to tell it." . . .

[Nanna recounts what her noble guest told her of horrors perpetrated during the sack of Rome.]

NANNA: . . . Now back to our story. The lady, snared by the bird lime with which love had smeared the baron's presence and manner, was all aflame; and her heart slithered up and down in her breast as if it were made of quicksilver. And thinking of the great honor of his ilk and the great deeds she imagined he had done on that terrible night, she twisted and turned on her bed like a person who has a freezing, burning passion; and since the blabber's face and words were tightly fixed in her head, it wrecked her sleep. And the very next morning, when Messer Sun's colors had painted Mistress Aurora's cheeks, she went to see her sister; and after hastily reeling off a snatch of a dream, she said: "What do you think of the pilgrim who has come here? Have you ever seen a handsomer man? Imagine the miracles he must have performed with arms in hand when they were fighting for Rome? He must surely be of noble birth; and certainly if I hadn't, after the death of my first consort, made a vow to remain a widow, I might even be led to make the same mistake again, but only with him. And certainly, sister I do not conceal the fact, indeed I swear it on the new affection I bear the noble foreigner, that since he died my heart has been bereft of love, and now I begin again to sense the signs of the ancient flame, which once consumed me in a trice, and not gradually. But before I do anything that is not decent and respectable may the earth open and swallow me alive, or a lightning bolt from the sky fling me into the abyss. I shall not rip up the laws of honor: he who had my love bore it off with him to the other world, and he will enjoy it there *in secolorum secula* [for all eternity]." And after saying these words, she began to wail so loudly that you would have thought she had been beaten.

PIPPA: Poor woman.

NANNA: Her sister, who wasn't a hypocrite and took things straight on, mocked her oath and her tears and answered her by saying: "Is it possible that you do not want to learn how sweet it is to make babies, and how honeyed are the gifts of Madonna Venus? What madness of yours is this? Do you think that the souls of the dead haven't better things to think about than whether their widows will marry again or not? But I want you to earn this victory of not having stooped to taking one of the many princes who wanted you. Do you want to fight with that floozy Cupid? You fool, don't do it, because you'll end up with a broken head; besides, all your neighbors are your enemies. You should know how to recognize good fortune, which has put its forelock in your hand; and just imagine, if our blood mixes with Roman blood, what city can compete with us? Now let's have prayers said in all the monasteries so that heaven will lead us to fortune. In the meanwhile it should be easy to keep him here; and perhaps he will be glad of it, since he is broken and forlorn, and then too because of the harshness of the cold which blows out of the heart of winter." And do you want to know the rest, Pippa? She sang vespers so effectively that she strangled her vows and respectability. My lady flung her honor over her shoulder, so that whether she was staying or going she saw and heard the baron. Night came, and when the crickets finally slept, she was still awake, tossing from side to side, talking to herself about him, burning with an anguish that only a person who goes to bed and gets up as the passion hammer commands can understand. And to be quite clear about it, her soul was compromised, and she came to an evil end with our friend: she did it, my daughter.

PIPPA: Wisely.

NANNA: No, stupidly.

PIPPA: Why?

NANNA: Because figured music says that

To him who nourishes a cold serpent in his breast
Will happen what happens to the clodhopper;
When he has made it warm and healthy,
It will then pay him with its venom.

5

Reformation Voices

20

ALFONSO DE VALDÉS

Dialogue of Lactancio and an Archdeacon, with a Rebuttal Letter from Baltasar Castiglione

1528

Alfonso de Valdés (ca. 1490–1532), a Renaissance scholar deeply influenced by the writings of his friend Desiderius Erasmus (Document 21), served as Latin secretary to Holy Roman Emperor Charles V. His service to Charles V included negotiations with Martin Luther's collaborator, the theologian Philipp Melanchthon, for a reconciliation between Catholics and Protestants. This effort ended abruptly with Valdés's death during an outbreak of plague in Vienna.

As a result of his intellectual bent as well as his political position, Valdés was uniquely able to propose an alternative view to Luigi Guicciardini's assessment of the sack of Rome (Document 16). The dialogue excerpted here is unabashedly one-sided; it mitigates the horrors perpetrated by the imperial invaders and blames Rome's defeat and desecration on papal corruption and indifference to Christianity's true values.

Valdés's family was rumored to be of Jewish origin, a matter that gained the attention of Baltasar (Baldassare) Castiglione (1478–1529), Pope Clement VII's nuncio to Spain. Castiglione, who is best known today as the author of The Book of the Courtier, *unleashed a viciously anti-Semitic attack on Valdés, part of which is included below. Castiglione wanted Valdés's manuscript burned and the author tried by the Inquisi-*

Alfonso de Valdés, *Dialogue of Lactancio and an Archdeacon,* trans. John Longhurst (Albuquerque: University of New Mexico Press, 1952), 20, 22–26, 31, 34–35 for the Valdés selection and 104–5, 109, 115 for excerpts from Castiglione's letter.

tion and perhaps denounced in some way by Emperor Charles V. None of these things happened, although only death from the plague saved Valdés from the inquisitorial process the Dominicans instituted against him. His book was placed on the church's Index of Prohibited Books.

A young cavalier of the court of the Emperor, named Lactancio [hereinafter LACT], met by chance in the plaza at Valladolid an archdeacon [hereinafter ARCH] returning from Rome in a soldier's dress. Entering the church of Saint Francis, they talk about recent occurrences in Rome. In the first part of the dialogue Lactancio explains to the archdeacon why the Emperor is not to blame for the affair; in the second part he shows that God permitted the whole thing for the good of Christianity. . . .

ARCH: Judging from your question, you don't know the whole story. I tell you there is no longer a man in Rome who dares to appear in the streets in ecclesiastical garb.

LACT: I can't believe it!

ARCH: When I left Rome the persecution of the clergy was so intense that no one would dare walk in the streets in the habit of a priest or friar.

LACT: Oh great God, how incomprehensible are Your judgments! Tell me, sir, were you in Rome when the army of the Emperor entered?

ARCH: Indeed I was—worse luck! I was there; in fact I was ruined there. And all I have left is what you see.

LACT: Why didn't you join the Spanish soldiers and save your possessions?

ARCH: Fortune was against me. I ran into some Germans and was lucky to escape with my life.

LACT: Do you mean to say it's true, what we hear from Rome and what they're talking about around here?

ARCH: I don't know what they write from Rome nor what they say around here, but I can tell you it's the most terrible thing any man has ever seen. I don't know how you feel about it here, although you don't seem particularly concerned, but on my word of honor I don't see how God can tolerate such things. If we were somewhere else, where it would be safe to talk, I'd have plenty more to say on the subject . . .

LACT: I won't tell a soul.

ARCH: Then see here, friend Lactancio, do you think it's a matter for celebration that the Emperor has perpetrated in Rome a crime worse than anything the infidels ever committed? Do you think it's right that to vent his personal anger, and in his desire for revenge, he has tried to destroy the Apostolic See, with the greatest display of infamy, disrespect and cruelty ever seen or heard of?

When the Goths took Rome, they didn't touch the church of St. Peter or the relics of the saints, or anything sacred. Those half-Christians had at least that much respect. But *our* Christians—if you can call them that—haven't even spared churches, monasteries or sanctuaries. They have violated, plundered, and profaned everything. I'm amazed that the earth doesn't swallow them up, along with the one man responsible for it all.

What do you think the Turks, Moors, Jews, and Lutherans will say, knowing that the head of Christianity has been mistreated in such fashion? Oh God, that You should tolerate such a thing! That You should permit such wickedness! Is this the kind of protection the Apostolic See should expect from its defender? Is this the honor Spain should expect from her powerful king? Is this the glory, happiness, and prosperity for which all Christianity was hoping? Is this why the Emperor's grandparents were given the title *Catholic Kings?* Why so many kingdoms and dominions were united under one ruler? Why he was elected Emperor? Is this why the Roman pontiffs helped him throw the French out of Italy, so that in one day he would tear down everything his predecessors had built up, with so much labor and over such a long period of years? So many churches, monasteries, and hospitals, devoted to the service and honor of God, now lie destroyed and violated! So many altars, and even the very church of the Prince of the Apostles, bathed in blood! And the many relics stolen and profaned by sacrilegious hands!

Was it for this that the Emperor's predecessors concentrated so much holiness in that city? Is this why they honored the churches by giving them so many relics? Why they gave so many gold and silver ornaments to the churches? Did they do all this so that he might come, with clean hands, to rob, to undo, and to destroy everything? Almighty God! Can such cruelty, such an affront, such abominable audacity, such a frightful deed, such execrable impiety go without harsh and exemplary punishment? I don't know how you feel about it here but, if you have *any* feelings on the subject, I don't see how you can conceal them as you do.

LACT: I've listened carefully to everything you've said and, as a matter of fact, although I've heard many people talk about this affair, I have never heard anyone condemn it as bitterly as you do. It seems to me you are very poorly informed and I suspect it is not reason but the shock of losing your possessions which makes you so bitter.

If I were to reply to you in the tone of personal passion that you have used, we would get nowhere. I prefer to discuss this calmly and to appeal to your discretion and judgment, so that before we part you will see how mistaken you have been. Just listen carefully and ask any questions you like so that we can clear things up as we go along.

ARCH: Go right ahead. But you're a better man than Cicero if you can make out a case for the Emperor in this business.

LACT: There's so much evidence in the Emperor's favor that anyone who couldn't make out a good case for him would be an absolute fool. First, I'll show you why the Emperor is not to blame for what happened in Rome. Second, I'll show you that it was God's judgment which brought about the punishment of that city. God realized that the Christian religion was being disgraced by the incredible wickedness practiced so widely there. He intended that Christendom should wake up and clean house so that we could live again like the Christians we're so proud to be.

ARCH: What a job you've given yourself! I don't think you'll convince me.

LACT: Let me make it clear at the start that nothing I say is intended to reflect on the office or person of the Pope, for of course his position should be respected by everyone. I couldn't speak ill of his person, in any case, because I realize none of this was his doing, really. He just had the wrong people around him. But to be sure that we understand each other, since the dispute concerns the Pope and the Emperor, tell me, what are the functions of the Pope and the Emperor, and what is the purpose behind their offices?

ARCH: My feeling is that the Emperor's duty is to defend his subjects, to keep them at peace, and to dispense justice by rewarding the good and punishing the wicked.

LACT: Well said. And the Pope?

ARCH: His duties are not so easy to define. They were not quite the same in St. Peter's time as they are today.

LACT: When I speak of the duties of the Pope, I mean those duties as they were conceived by the Founder of that office.

ARCH: My understanding is that the papal office was established so that the Pope might explain Holy Scripture and teach Christian doctrine to the world. This he would do both in word and in deed. With tears and prayer he would beg God's blessing for all Christians. He would have the power to absolve all penitent sinners and to proclaim the damnation of those who obstinately persisted in their evil ways. His constant endeavor would be to see that peace and harmony reign among Christians. And finally, as the supreme pontiff on earth he would provide a living example of the holiness of Jesus Christ, our Redeemer. Since the human heart is more easily moved by actions than by words, it is especially important that he set this example. That's what I understand from Scripture. Tell me if I have overlooked anything.

LACT: You have the general idea. Just remember what you have said, because we'll come back to it after a while.

ARCH: I won't forget.

LACT: You have told me the duties of the Emperor and the Pope. Now, if I can show you that Rome's destruction was caused by the Emperor's devotion to duty and the Pope's neglect of duty, whom would you blame?

ARCH: If you can prove that—but I don't see how you can—then I would have to blame the Pope for the sack of Rome.

LACT: You said that the Pope should provide a living example of Jesus Christ. Well now, what do you think Jesus Christ would prefer? To maintain peace or provoke war?

ARCH: Obviously the Author of peace considers nothing more abominable than war.

LACT: Then if a person supports war instead of peace, how can he be a follower of Jesus Christ?

ARCH: It would be impossible. But what are you getting at? . . .

LACT: The Pope is supposed to be a living example of all Christian virtue. He is supposed to keep peace and harmony among us, even at the risk of his life. That's why I'm amazed that he should want to wage war just to get the very things that Jesus Christ told us to scorn. And he even finds among Christians some who will help him in such nefarious work, so damaging to the honor of Christ. . . . [Lactanzio relates the atrocities against fellow Christian civilians committed by papal forces in the decades of war preceding the sack of Rome, which he says "went beyond the emperors Nero and Dionysius of Syracuse, and all other cruel tyrants who have ever reigned." He cites in horror the reports of pregnant women cut open and their babies roasted before their eyes.]

What Jew, Turk, Moor or other infidel will want to accept Jesus Christ when His Vicar sponsors such deeds? Who will want to serve or honor Him? Those Christians who cannot read the teachings of Christ have no choice but to follow His Vicar. And if everyone imitates His Vicar, who will want to live among Christians?

Do you think that this is the way to imitate Jesus Christ? Do you think the Christian public is edified by such actions? Do you think that Holy Scripture teaches us to behave this way? Do you think this is the way the shepherd should watch over his flock? Do you think these are the works of the true Vicar of Jesus Christ? Do you think that this office was established as an agency for the destruction of Christendom?

ARCH: I agree that all those things are very cruel, but the people of Italy would look down on a pope who didn't wage war. They would think it a great insult if a single inch of Church land were lost.

LACT: There are any number of ways to reply to that but, to save time, let's assume the impossible should happen. Suppose the Emperor tried to take the Church lands from the Pope. Wouldn't it be better for the Pope to lose all his temporal power than to keep it at the expense of Christian suffering and dishonor to Jesus Christ?

ARCH: Certainly not. Would you be willing to see the Church despoiled?

LACT: What do you mean, despoiled? Whom are you referring to when you talk about the Church?

ARCH: The Pope and the cardinals.

LACT: How about all the other Christians? Don't they make up the Church, too?

ARCH: So they say.

LACT: Then the strength and authority of the Church lie in its membership and not in its political power. Consequently, the larger the membership, the greater is the Church. To reduce the number of Christians is to despoil the Church.

ARCH: It seems that way to me.

LACT: Then anyone responsible for the death of a Christian does more harm to the Church of Jesus Christ than he who deprives the Roman pontiff of his temporal power.

ARCH: That could be.

LACT: Now about this war which you say the Pope began merely to protect the papal state. Forgetting for the moment all the other evils, how many people do you suppose have died since this war began?

ARCH: An infinite number.

LACT: Then the Pope has done more to despoil God's Church than anyone who might try to reduce the temporal power of the Church. If someone should try to take away Christ's cloak, do you think He would fight to hold on to it?

ARCH: No.

LACT: If the Pope's function is to imitate Jesus Christ, how can you justify his resorting to violence to keep what he has?

ARCH: If people knew the Pope wouldn't fight, the Church would soon
  lose everything it had.
LACT: It's not for me to decide whether it's so necessary for popes to
  have temporal power . . .

[Baltasar Castiglione to Alfonso de Valdés, written sometime after
August 1528 and before Castiglione's death on February 2, 1529.]

You also attempt to prove that the outrages inflicted on Rome were the
judgment of God. You base your allegation on a deprecation of all the
things which you claim were being done in Rome. You speak of the
many deceptions and falsehoods there, as well as the lack of religion
among clergy men. You scold those who worship the relics of the saints,
the images of Christ and of the glorious Virgin Our Lady, and claim that
by use of these things the priests take advantage of the ignorant and
simple in order to make money out of the adoration of false relics. . . .

I notice also that you like to use pleasant-sounding insinuations in
your book. You say, for example, that the saints, who did not care for
worldly things during their lifetimes, probably liked to see their remains
despoiled of that which they disdained while alive. This mockery of
yours strikes me as rather stale and unbecoming a good Christian. . . .

Only you and your ilk rejoiced at the harsh persecution of the Pope
and the Italians, even when the dumb beasts and the very stones showed
pain and sorrow at the world-wide destruction you are trying to insti-
gate. No doubt you wanted to imitate the knavish words of those perfidi-
ous Jews who, in order to induce Pilate to sentence our Savior to death,
said to him, "If thou let this man go, thou art not Caesar's friend." . . .

Do not think that by your hypocrisies you have deceived those who
can easily suspect in you the roots of errors of your [Jewish] forebears.
No respect is due you, since you have thus revealed yourself. The honorable inquisitors shall not fail in their duties—those inquisitors whom
you have called Pharisees at the beginning of your dialogue, whom you
have described as full of superstitions, because you know in advance
that they will pronounce "false judgments" on you and your work. I tell
you they will pronounce a true sentence upon you. And Jesus Christ will
not come forth to protect you, because He does not protect His enemies,
but punishes ill will with the sword of divine justice.

21

DESIDERIUS ERASMUS

Julius Excluded from Heaven: A Dialogue
1514
and
Selections from Letters
1514–1522

Desiderius Erasmus (1466?–1536), one of the most influential Renaissance thinkers who remained in the Catholic fold, came to Rome for the first time in February 1509. His visit to Italy had begun in Turin in 1506, when at the age of forty he served as tutor to Giovanni and Bernardo Boerio, the two sons of the personal physician of English King Henry VII. Erasmus did not write specifically about the places he visited or the people he met in Rome or anywhere else in Italy. But scholars widely agree that his most famous essay, "In Praise of Folly," conceived as he traveled on horseback across the Alps, reflects his acerbic judgment on what he had recently witnessed in Rome.

"Julius Excluded," a savage critique of Pope Julius II, is more explicit. It was immediately and widely attributed to Erasmus, and he neither denied nor admitted its authorship. As the dialogue opens, Pope Julius II, goaded by his evil guardian spirit, Genius, is at St. Peter's Gate, engaged in a verbal dispute with St. Peter, who bars the doors to Paradise. After some idle chitchat, St. Peter and Julius get to the crux of the matter: Julius's demand for a place in heaven is about to be denied. The essay holds an important place in the corpus of writings by critics of Roman Catholic practices who remained loyal to the church, even as other religious thinkers took the path that led to the Protestant Reformation. Following this excerpt are selections from Erasmus's correspondence in the years after he left Rome, in which he unfailingly expresses nostalgia for his stay, reminding us of the qualities of Renaissance Rome that

Collected Works of Erasmus (Toronto: University of Toronto Press, 1976 ff.), vol. 27, 191–93 for "Julius Excluded" and vol. 3, 93–94; vol. 5, 197–98; vol. 8, 151; and vol. 9, 144–45 for letters.

attracted visitors by the hundreds of thousands each year. He contrasts
the pagan world of ancient Rome with what he deems to be the superior
virtues of Christian Rome.

Julius Excluded

JULIUS: Ah, now you're coming to it: listen. The church, once poor and
   starving, is now enriched with every possible ornament.

PETER: What ornaments? Warm faith?

JULIUS: You're talking nonsense again.

PETER: Sacred learning?

JULIUS: You don't give up, do you?

PETER: Contempt for the world?

JULIUS: Allow me to explain. I'm talking about real ornaments, not mere
   words like those.

PETER: What then?

JULIUS: Royal palaces, the most handsome horses and mules, hordes of
   servants, well-trained troops, dainty courtiers . . .

GENIUS: . . . delicious harlots, groveling pimps . . .

JULIUS: . . . gold, purple, taxes; in fact, such is the wealth and splendor of
   the Roman pontiff that, by comparison, any king would seem a poor
   and insignificant fellow; any man, however ambitious, would admit
   defeat; any man, however extravagant, would condemn his own fru-
   gality; and any rich man—a money-lender, even—would look with
   envy on our wealth. These, I tell you, are the ornaments that I have
   protected and increased.

PETER: But tell me, who was the first to burden and defile the church
   with these ornaments of yours, when Christ intended it to be wholly
   pure and wholly unencumbered by such things?

JULIUS: What's that got to do with it? The important thing is that we
   have them to possess and to enjoy. However, they do say that someone called Constantine transferred the whole majesty of his empire
   to the Roman pontiff Sylvester [the document by which Constantine
   donated his empire to the papacy was definitively determined to be
   a forgery by Lorenzo Valla in 1440]: his horses, trappings, chariots,
   helmet, belt, cloak, guards, swords, golden crowns (very fine gold
   too), armies, artillery, cities, kingdoms.

PETER: Are there any reliable records of this splendid gift?

JULIUS: Nothing but one interpolation included among the decretals
   [papal decrees].

PETER: Perhaps it's all a hoax.

JULIUS: I sometimes think that myself. What sane man would give up such a magnificent empire, even to his father? But it pleases us greatly to believe it, and we've used threats to impose absolute silence on the snoopers who try to disprove it.

PETER: You still talk of nothing but the world.

JULIUS: You must still be dreaming of that ancient church in which, with a few starving bishops, you yourself, a pontiff shivering with cold, were exposed to poverty, sweat, dangers, and a thousand other trials. But now time has changed everything for the better. Now the Roman pontiff is something very different; you were pontiff in name and title only. Ah, if only you could see today the holy temples built for a king's ransom, the thousands of clerics in every country, most of them with enormous incomes, the bishops rivaling the greatest kings with their armies and wealth, the clerics' magnificent palaces! If you could only see, in particular, life in Rome today: all the cardinals in purple, attended by whole regiments of retainers, the horses more than fit for a king, the mules decked in fine cloth, gold and jewels, some even shod with gold and silver! If you could catch a glimpse of the supreme pontiff, carried aloft in a golden chair on the shoulders of his men, while the people on all sides pay homage at a wave of his hand; if you could hear the thunder of the cannon, the blare of the cornets, the blasting of the horns, see the flashes of the guns, and hear the applause of the people, the cheers, the whole scene lit by gleaming torches, even the greatest princes barely permitted to kiss the blessed feet; if you could watch the selfsame Roman priest, on foot this time, placing the golden crown on the head of the Roman emperor, who is the king of all kings (if written laws mean anything: in fact, he receives merely the shadow of a great name); if, I say, you could see and hear all this, what would you say?

PETER: That I was looking at a tyrant worse than any in the world, the enemy of Christ, the bane of the church.

JULIUS: You'd change your tune if you'd witnessed even one of my triumphs, such as my entry into Bologna, my celebrations at Rome after the defeat of Venice, my return to Rome after fleeing Bologna, or the most recent one after the totally unexpected rout of the French at Ravenna; if you'd seen the ponies, the horses, the columns of armed soldiers, the panoply of the generals, the displays of hand-picked boys, the torches gleaming on all sides, the sumptuous litters, the procession of bishops, the stately cardinals, the trophies, the spoils; if you'd heard the cheers of people and soldiers resounding to the sky, the sound of applause echoing all round, the music of trumpets, the thunder of cornets, and seen the flashes of cannon, the coins thrown to the people, and myself, the leader and prime mover of the whole pageant, carried on high like some god: then you'd call the Scipios, the Aemilii, and the Augusti miserable skinflints compared with me.

PETER: Whoa! that's enough triumphs, General Braggart! I'd welcome those men, for all they were pagans, out of disgust for you, the most holy Father in Christ who celebrated triumphs after the slaughter of thousands of Christians for your sake, who caused the ruin of so many armies, who never won a single soul for Christ by word or by example. There's fatherly affection for you! O worthy vicar of the Christ who gave himself to save all men, while you have engineered the ruin of the whole world to save you own pestilent head!

[The dialogue continues but St. Peter does not relent, and the unrepentant Julius storms off to gather an army for a future attack on St. Peter's Gate.]

Selections from Letters

[May 15, 1515, to Domenico Grimani, Cardinal of St. Mark's Cathedral in Venice and one of Erasmus's patrons in Rome.]

A deep regret for Rome is inescapable, when I think of its great store of great advantages available together. First of all, the bright light, the noble setting of the most famous city in the world, the delightful freedom, the many richly furnished libraries, the sweet society of all those great scholars, all the literary conversations, all the monuments of antiquity, and not least so many leading lights of the world gathered together in one place. In particular, whenever I bethink me of the remarkable favor shown me by other cardinals, and especially by his eminence of Nantes, the most cordial encouragement of the cardinal of Bologna, and from the cardinal of San Giorgio, not merely encouragement but generosity quite out of the common; above all, the most promising conversation with your Eminence—all this makes me feel that no fortune could possibly fall to my lot generous enough to wean my heart from its longing for the Rome which I once tasted.

[November 13, 1517, to Domenico Grimani.]

Let Rome prepare a welcome, therefore, for the first or at least the greatest teacher of her religion. Let her embrace the herald of her ancient fame, let her return the love of one who loved a city he had never seen. Happy indeed the change in the style of her prosperity! Long ago under imperial despots she offered worship to dumb images; now under Peter and Paul she presides over the earth. Long ago the handmaid of every superstition, now she is the great mistress of true religion. Jove on the Capitol has made way for Christ, who alone is best and greatest; the emperor for Peter and Paul, immeasurably gifted each of them in his own way; that solemn famous senate for the College of Cardinals, revered all the world over. If she is stirred by arch or pyramid, the relics of her ancient superstition, how can she resist the monuments of revealed religion to be found in the books of the apostles? She marvels at Hadrian's statue or Domitian's baths; let her embrace instead the most holy epistles of Peter and Paul. If she loves to read in the works of a Sallust or a Livy the ancient fables of her early days, how she was exalted from small beginnings to a world dominion that was soon to fall, guided by vultures, much more ought she to love the writings of the apostles and evangelists, in which she can recognize from what rudiments she rose to a dominion over the church that shall never fail, guided by Christ. Among the Jews not a trace remains today of their temple, once so sacred; so too the Capitol of Rome, which foolish prophets long ago promised should be eternal, has left so few remnants that one cannot even point out where it stood.

If she admires the tongue of Cicero, of which it were hard to say whether it did more good or harm to the republic, why does she not enjoy still more the eloquence of Paul, to which she owes the greatest part of her salvation and religion? She was always greedy for praise, and now she has this great and famous herald of her glory, for what triumph so great as to be praised in the words of an apostle? O Romans, Romans, learn what Paul did for you, and you will understand what the glories are that you must maintain. Listen to his warning voice, lest you fail to know what you must shun. He praises faith, which nowhere else has kept more spotless. He speaks of obedience, which made you early exchange superstition for religion. He grants you affability, whose companion often is credulity; this was the reason why false apostles tempted you into Judaism; but with that ease of manners went prudence, which caused a swift repentance. He marks your proud spirit and therefore warns you so carefully against pride and insolence, calls you from luxury to sobriety of life, from lust to chastity, from brutality to toleration, from strife to concord, from war to peace. Such is your true Roman character, from which it would be disgraceful to descend. Beware lest you, being Rome, degenerate into Babylon.

[January 28, 1521, to Arkleb of Boskovice, governor of Moravia.]

I know well enough the complaints that are commonly directed against the see of Rome; but just as it is unwise to give immediate credence to popular rumor, so it is clearly unfair to blame the pope for everything that happens in Rome. Much is done without his knowledge, for one man cannot know everything; much that he dislikes, and against opposition from him. And in the present posture of human affairs, if Peter himself were to preside in Rome, he would be compelled, I suspect, to connive at some things which in his heart of hearts he could not possibly approve.

[August 1, 1522, to Pope Adrian VI (r. 1522–1523).]

It was not difficult to foresee, most holy Father, with what an ostentatious outburst of delight Rome was likely to welcome the arrival of one who is by far the most popular of popes, and especially as she has now longed for so many months for his arrival. And so I sought for some way in which, amidst the rejoicing of so many thousands, amidst all those cheering and applauding crowds, amidst the blare of trumpets and the thunder of cannon, you might hear the small voice of a man of lowly estate and one moreover who lives far off, and thus might recognize that your Erasmus was not wholly silent; for just as he listened long ago to your teaching as a theologian and admired you for your nobility of character, so now he is a humble sheep in the flock of which you are the apostolic shepherd.

22

MARTIN LUTHER

Table Talk

ca. 1525–1539

Much controversy surrounds Martin Luther's (1483–1546) pilgrim-
age to Rome late in 1510, especially about how what he saw and heard
may have influenced his later thinking. Surely he was horrified by the
public spectacle of the unseemly indulgence-hawkers and hustlers of fake
relics who interfered with his penitential visits to Rome's holy sites. The
balance of scholarly opinion, however, is that his experience as a traveler
did not lead in a powerful and direct way to his posting in 1517 of the
Ninety-Five Theses that began the Protestant Reformation. There is more
to Protestant religious differences with Catholics than one particularly
unhappy tourist on a pilgrimage. Nor does Lutheran theology depend on
a sinful clergy for its justification. Still, there can be no doubt that Martin
Luther remembered his Rome pilgrimage with profound distaste, increas-
ingly so as the years went by and he came to see the pope as an Antichrist.

The excerpts below allow for an independent judgment. They come
from the Table Talk *of Martin Luther, a collection of words presum-*
ably spoken by him and taken down at various times by his friends and
close associates, mostly at mealtimes in the years after his marriage
in 1525. These circumstances raise significant issues about the reli-
ability of memory as well as about the accuracy of notes recorded by
friends and students. Moreover, the account about the Jew in Wittenberg
(DCCCLXIX, p. 145) so closely parallels Boccaccio's tale (Document 1)
as to suggest that this is either a stunning interplay of fiction in 1350 and
fact two centuries later, or perhaps some jocular storytelling by Martin
Luther based consciously or not on his familiarity with Boccaccio's story.
As fact or fiction, the conversations challenge the historian's ability to
employ complex evidence in ways that provide deeper understanding of
Renaissance and Reformation Rome.

William Hazlitt, trans. and ed., *The Table Talk of Martin Luther* (London: George Bell and Sons, 1890), 85, 199, 205, 207, 208, 210, 216, 219, 224, 283, 286, 353, 362. The Roman numerals for the various sections are from this edition.

CXCIV

At Rome was a Church called Pantheon, where were collected effigies of all the gods they were able to bring together out of the whole world. All these could well accord one with another, for the devil therewith jeered the world, laughing in his fist; but when Christ came, him they could not endure, but all the devils, idols, and heretics grew stark mad and full of rage; for he, the right and true God and man, threw them altogether on a heap. The pope also sets himself powerfully against Christ, but he must likewise be put to confusion and destroyed.

CCCCXLIV

They show, at Rome, the head of St. John the Baptist, though 'tis well known that the Saracens opened his tomb, and burned his remains to ashes. These impostures of the papists cannot be too seriously reprehended.

CCCCLIX

The pope's crown is named *regnum mundi,* the kingdom of the world. I have heard it credibly reported at Rome, that this crown is worth more than all the princedoms of Germany. God placed Popedom in Italy not without cause, for the Italians can make out many things to be real and true, which in truth are not so: they have crafty and subtle brains.

CCCCLXVI

A German, making his confession to a priest at Rome, promised, on oath, to keep secret whatsoever the priest should impart unto him, until he reached home; whereupon the priest gave him a leg of the ass on which Christ rode into Jerusalem, very neatly bound up in silk, and said: This is the holy relic on which the Lord Christ corporally did sit, with his sacred legs touching this ass's leg. Then was the German wondrous glad, and carried the said holy relic with him into Germany. When he got to the borders, he bragged of his holy relic in the presence of four others, his comrades, when, lo! it turned out that each of them had likewise received from the same priest a leg, after promising the same secrecy. Thereupon, all exclaimed, with great wonder: Lord! had that ass five legs?

CCCCLXX

The pope and his crew can in nowise endure the idea of reformation; the mere word creates more alarm at Rome, than thunderbolts from heaven, or the day of judgment. A cardinal said, the other day: Let them eat, and drink, and do what they will; but as to reforming us, we think that is a vain idea; we will not endure it. Neither will we protestants be satisfied, though they administer the sacrament in both kinds, and permit priests to marry; we will also have the doctrine of the faith pure and unfalsified, and the righteousness that justifies and saves before God, and which expels and drives away all idolatry and false-worshipping; these gone and banished, the foundation on which Popedom is built falls also.

CCCCLXXIII

When I was in Rome a disputation was openly held, at which were present thirty learned doctors besides myself, against the pope's power; he boasting, that with his right hand he commands the angels in heaven, and with his left draws souls out of purgatory, and that his person is mingled with the godhead. Calixtus disputed against these assertions, and showed that it was only on earth that power was given to the pope to bind and to loose. The other doctors hereupon assailed him with exceeding vehemence, and Calixtus discontinued his arguments, saying, he had only spoken by way of disputation, and that his real opinions were far otherwise.

CCCCXCII

The covetousness of the popes has exceeded all others, for the devil made choice of Rome as his peculiar habitation. The ancients said: Rome is a den of covetousness, a root of all wickedness. I have also read in a very old book, this verse following:

"Versus Amor, mundi caput est, et bestia terræ."

That is, when the word Amor is turned and read backward, *Roma,* Rome, the head of the world, a beast that devours all lands. At Rome, all is raked to their hands without preaching or church service, by superstition, idolatry, and selling their good works to the poor ignorant laity for money. St. Peter describes such covetousness with express and clear words, when he says: "They have a heart exercised with covetous practices." I am persuaded a man cannot know the disease of covetousness, unless he know Rome; for the deceits and jugglings in other parts are nothing in comparison with those at Rome.

CCCCXCVIII

Luther, coming from Rome, showed the prince elector of Saxony a picture he had brought with him, whereon was painted how the pope had fooled the whole world with his superstitions and idolatries. There was the little ship of the church, as they term it, almost filled with friars, monks, and priests, casting lines out of the ship to those that were in the sea; the pope, with the cardinals and bishops, sat behind, in the end of the ship, overshadowed and covered by the Holy Ghost, who was looking up towards heaven, and through whom those swimming in the sea, in great danger of their lives, were hoisted up into the ship and saved.

These and like fooleries we then believed as articles of faith. The papists blind people by pretending that they go through much tribulation in this world; whereas they wallow in all the glory, pleasures, and delights of the earth. But let them be assured, that ere many years the power of their abominable blasphemies, idolatries, and damnable religion, will be broken, if not destroyed.

And on the contrary, we, who for the sake of confessing God's holy Word in truth, are terrified, banished, imprisoned, and slain here on earth by that man of sin, and God's enemy, the antichrist-pope of Rome, at the last day, with unspeakable comfort, shall take possession of the fruits of our assured hopes—namely, everlasting consolation, joy, and salvation.

DXIII

The ornaments and gay apparel used in Popedom, in celebrating mass, and other ceremonies, were partly taken out from Moses, and partly from the heathen. For as the priests saw that the public shows and plays, held in the market places, drew away the people, who took delight therein, they were moved to institute shows and plays in the churches, so as to draw children and unlearned people to church. Such are the toys they exhibit on Easter-eve, very pleasing and acceptable, not for devotion's sake, but to delight the foolish fancy.

DCLXXI

Erasmus of Rotterdam is the vilest miscreant that ever disgraced the earth. He made several attempts to draw me into his snares, and I should have been in danger, but that God lent me special aid. In 1525, he sent one of his doctors, with 200 Hungarian ducats, as a present to my wife; but I refused to accept them, and enjoined my wife to meddle not in these matters. He is a very Caiphas.

DCLXXIX

Erasmus was poisoned at Rome and at Venice with epicurean doctrines [from the Greek philosopher Epicurus]. He extols the Arians more highly than the Papists; he ventured to say that Christ is named God but once in St. John, where Thomas says: "My Lord and my God." His chief doctrine is, we must carry ourselves according to the time, or, as the proverb goes, hang the cloak according to the wind; he only looked to himself, to have good and easy days, and so died like an epicurean, without any one comfort of God.

DCCCLXIX

A Jew came to me at Wittenberg, and said: He was desirous to be baptized, and made a Christian, but that he would first go to Rome to see the chief head of Christendom. From this intention, myself, Philip[p] Melanc[h]thon, and other divines, labored to dissuade him, fearing lest, when he witnessed the offenses and knaveries at Rome, he might be scared from Christendom. But the Jew went to Rome, and when he had sufficiently seen the abominations acted there, he returned to us again, desiring to be baptized, and said: Now I will willingly worship the God of the Christians, for he is a patient God. If he can endure such wickedness and villainy as is done at Rome, he can suffer and endure all the vices and knaveries of the world.

DCCCLXXXVIII

[Pietro] Bembo, an exceeding learned man, who had thoroughly investigated Rome, said: Rome is a filthy, stinking puddle, full of the wickedest wretches in the world.

DCCCLXXXIX

In the time of Leo X, there were in an Augustine convent at Rome two monks, who revolted at the horrible wickedness of the papists, and, in their sermons, found fault with the pope. In the night, two assassins were introduced into their cells, and next morning they were found dead, their tongues cut out, and stuck on their backs. Whoso in Rome is heard to speak against the pope, either gets a sound *strappado* [medieval torture associated with the Inquisition] or has his throat cut; for the pope's name is *Noli me tangere* [Touch me not, John 20:17].

DCCCXC

When I was at Rome, they showed me, for a precious holy relic, the halter wherewith Judas hanged himself. Let us bear this in mind, and consider in what ignorance our forefathers were.

23

CASPAR SCHOPPE

Letter to Conrad Rittershausen on Giordano Bruno

February 8, 1600

Early in 1593 the Roman Inquisition brought Giordano Bruno under its direct jurisdiction, forcibly taking him from the Venetian inquisitors who had arrested him the previous year but whom papal authorities feared might be too lenient in sentencing him. Friar Giordano, who had been ordained as a Dominican monk, had long been accused of holding suspicious opinions and of possessing heretical books, including the writings of Erasmus (Document 21). He had abandoned the Dominican order years earlier to take up the life of a wandering scholar, residing variously in France, Geneva, England, Germany, Bohemia, and Venice. Always a troubled individual, wherever he went he managed to dissipate his initially enthusiastic welcome.

Bruno published numerous books on Copernican astronomy, mathematics, philosophy, and theology, none of them acceptable to Roman church authorities. For seven years, as the inquisitors ever so slowly gathered evidence, he remained locked in Tor di Nona, the papal prison along

---

Luigi Firpo, *Il Processo di Giordano Bruno* (Naples: Edizione Scientifiche Italiane, 1949), 104–5.

the Tiber where Benvenuto Cellini (Document 18) had been imprisoned years earlier. Then the church made a final decision to turn him over to Rome's civilian government, with instructions that his punishment should not involve the shedding of blood. This euphemism meant that he would be burned at the stake, a sentence carried out nine days later, on February 17, 1600, in Campo dei Fiori (Field of Flowers), the square near Piazza Navona commonly used for public executions.

The church's official condemnation took place at the house of Cardinal Madruzzi adjacent to the church of Santa Agnese in Piazza Navona. Amid the large crowd assembled to watch was the young German scholar Caspar Schoppe (1576–1649), a former Lutheran who had recently converted to Catholicism. The excerpt below is from the letter he wrote to his former law professor at the university of Altdorf bei Nürnberg (Bavaria), Conrad Rittershausen, detailing what he saw and heard. Schoppe expressed dismay that the learned Bruno would sacrifice his life to defend the fourteen propositions read aloud by the papal notary on behalf of the nine Cardinal Inquisitors present at the occasion. But sacrifice Bruno did, giving eternal testimony to the tenacity with which Reformation Catholics and their opponents refused to tolerate each other's views. Along with the spectacle, the clerical corruption, and the tribulations of earning a living, such intolerance was a defining aspect of life in Renaissance Rome.

With its own mouth the Church declares that Bruno is an impenitent heretic, pertinacious and obstinate; he is condemned to degradation, expelled from the ecclesiastical Forum, and turned over to the Governor of Rome so that he can be punished appropriately. It is further ordered that all his writings shall be publically burned in Piazza Saint Peter and inserted in the Index of Prohibited Books.

   I. Negates transubstantiation [that the communion bread and wine are the actual body and blood of Christ].

   II. Casts doubt on the virginity of Mary [the mother of Christ].

   III. Lived in heretical countries and followed their customs.

   IV. Wrote the *Spaccio della Bestia trionfante* [The Expulsion of the Triumphant Beast] against the pope.

   V. Maintains the existence of innumerable and eternal worlds.

   VI. Asserts the doctrine of metempsychosis [Greek philosophical variant of reincarnation] and the possibility that a single soul can exist in two bodies.

VII. Holds that magic is good and legitimate.

VIII. Identifies the Holy Ghost as a worldly [not Divine] soul.

IX. Affirms that Moses simulated his miracles and invented the Ten Commandments.

X. Declares that the Bible is nothing but a dream.

XI. Holds that even devils will be saved.

XII. Opines the existence of men before Adam.

XIII. Asserts that Christ is not God but a trickster and a magician, and that his execution was rightful.

XIV. Asserts that the prophets and the apostles also were magicians and that almost all of them came to a bad end.

A Chronology of Renaissance Rome
(1300–1626)

1300s The papacy relocates from Rome to Avignon, France (1309–1377). Rome experiences a nadir lasting until the mid-fifteenth century, with civil warfare in the streets, ancient monuments in ruins, and the power of the medieval papacy a distant memory. Early Renaissance developments appear first in Florence and other Italian city-states, then in Rome.

1347–
1351 The Black Death, an outbreak of plague (primarily bubonic), kills as much as one-third of Europe's people.

Giovanni Boccaccio writes *The Decameron.*

1354 Radical popular leader Cola di Rienzo is assassinated by a Roman mob.

1377 Pope Gregory XI, at the urging of Saint Catherine of Siena, returns the papacy to Rome.

1378 The Western Schism begins with the election of an alternate pope, or antipope, who takes up residence in Avignon.

1417 The Western Schism ends with the election of Oddone Colonna, of the noble Roman Colonna family, as Pope Martin V.

1453 The execution of Stefano Porcaro and the triumph of Pope Nicholas V bring to an end more than a century of political chaos in Rome. The papacy establishes political supremacy over the city's governance, which lasts without interruption until the nineteenth century.

1471–
1484 Pope Sixtus IV initiates an artistic renaissance in Rome, restructuring the Campidoglio, building the Sistine Bridge, and constructing the Sistine Chapel. The Roman Academy formally reconvenes under papal sponsorship in 1478, thus reversing completely the antihumanist suspicions of Sixtus IV's predecessor, Pope Paul II.

1492   Christopher Columbus arrives in the New World.

Lorenzo Medici the Magnificent dies in Florence.

Roderic Llançol i Borja (Rodrigo Borgia) becomes Pope Alexander VI.

1494   King Charles VIII of France invades Italy, initiating a period of warfare in Italy that lasts more than half a century.

1506   Pope Julius II lays the cornerstone of the new St. Peter's Basilica and assigns Donato Bramante as chief architect.

1511   Raphael paints the *Portrait of Pope Julius II* shortly after completing the *School of Athens* in the Apostolic Palace of the Vatican.

1512   Michelangelo completes the Sistine Chapel ceiling with his portrayal of the Creation.

1517   Martin Luther posts his Ninety-Five Theses, among other charges denouncing the indulgences imposed to pay for the reconstruction of St. Peter's Basilica in Rome. This is the usual starting date assigned to the Protestant Reformation.

1526–
1527   Rome's people are enumerated in a household census taken in preparation for a feared invasion of the city.

1527   Holy Roman Emperor Charles V's troops invade and then sack the city of Rome.

1540   Ignatius of Loyola obtains papal approval for the new Society of Jesus, called the Jesuits, marking the beginning of the Catholic Reformation.

1541   Michelangelo completes his fresco *The Last Judgment* on the altar wall of the Sistine Chapel, but Catholic Reformation prelates find its nudity offensive and order veils to be painted onto the masterpiece.

1545–
1563   The Council of Trent meets to define Catholic Reformation doctrine.

1550   Giorgio Vasari coins the term *Renaissance* to describe the artistic movement centered in Florence beginning around 1300 in his publication of *Le Vite de' più eccellenti pittori, scultori, ed architettori (Lives of the Most Eminent Painters, Sculptors, and Architects)*.

1555   *July 14*   Pope Paul IV issues a bull confining the Jews to ghettos and severely restricting their economic activity.

September 25   Peace of Augsburg splits the Holy Roman Empire into Protestant and Catholic lands.

1559   Peace of Cateau-Cambrésis ends the Italian wars begun in 1494, leaving Spain as the dominant power on the peninsula.

1600 Giordano Bruno is condemned for heresy and burned at the stake in the Campo de' Fiori in Rome.

1610 Seventeen-year-old Artemisia Gentileschi paints *Susanna and the Elders.*

July 18 Caravaggio dies.

1626 St. Peter's Basilica, begun 120 years earlier, is officially dedicated.

Questions for Consideration

1. How would you characterize various contemporary opinions about Renaissance popes? What are the key differences in how they are presented in *The Decameron*, Alfonso de Valdès's *Dialogue*, Montaigne's *Travel Journal*, and Erasmus's *Julius Excluded*?

2. Compare and contrast the gender roles drawn in *La Lozana Andaluza* with those found in Cellini's *Autobiography* and in *Aretino's Dialogues*. In what ways do these generalizations survive into the present?

3. The sack of Rome in 1527 was arguably the most critical event in the history of Renaissance Rome. Compare the viewpoints of Luigi Guicciardini and Alfonso de Valdès on the impact of this disaster on the city.

4. What fascinated travelers who came to Renaissance Rome? What repelled them?

5. What role did public ritual play in Renaissance Rome?

6. Rome in the time of the Renaissance was a city of faith. However, the people also held fast to beliefs and assumptions with little or no support in official Christian dogma. Cite examples of such beliefs, and explain their coexistence with formally approved religious practices.

7. Is there a pattern to the reactions of visitors to Rome that might be linked to their places of origin? For example, did Englishmen see Rome differently than did Frenchmen?

8. What evidence of hostility to the papacy and the clergy do you find in the popular writings of Rome's people, especially in the pasquinades and carnival songs?

9. Several documents reflect virulently anti-Semitic practices and beliefs. Discuss the prevalence and impact of this hostility toward Jews.

10. In what ways does the study of Rome's street life contribute to a better understanding of popular culture more generally in Renaissance Europe?

11. Did the manifest corruption exhibited in Rome's daily life nurture the spread of the Protestant Reformation in significant ways? Explain.

12. What are the continuities and differences you observe in the ways elite and popular observers describe life in Renaissance Rome? Contrast, for example, du Bellay and Montaigne with Delicado and Petronio.

13. Historians are increasingly interested in what may be learned from household artifacts. From the inventory of Caravaggio's possessions and the more scattered references to ordinary goods by Cellini and Delicado, what can you reconstruct about the living conditions of ordinary Romans?

14. Which selection seems most objective in its depiction of Renaissance Rome, and which most biased? Why?

15. How do women's voices (Documents 3 and 11) differ from men's voices (Documents 18 and 19) in their assertions about Roman sexual norms? How does evidence in which the voice is ambiguous or uncertain (Documents 4, 5, 6, 7, 9, and 17) complicate your assessment?

16. Several of the sources comment on proper and improper behavior on the part of Roman women. What do they suggest about ideals of femininity in Renaissance Rome? Do these ideals differ according to social status?

Selected Bibliography

Birch, Debra J. *Pilgrimage to Rome in the Middle Ages: Continuity and Change.* Woodbridge, U.K.: Boydell Press, 1998.

Bonfil, Robert. *Jewish Life in Renaissance Italy,* trans. Anthony Oldcorn. Berkeley: University of California Press, 1994.

Burckhardt, Jacob. *The Civilization of the Renaissance in Italy,* trans. S. C. G. Middlemore. New York, 1950; orig. pub. Basel, 1860.

Celenza, Christopher S., and Gouwens, Kenneth, eds. *Humanism and Creativity in the Renaissance: Essays in Honor of Ronald G. Witt.* Leiden, Neth.: Brill, 2006.

Chamberlin, Eric R. *The Sack of Rome.* London: B. T. Batsford, 1979.

Chambers, David Sanderson. *Cardinal Bainbridge in the Court of Rome, 1509–1514.* London: Oxford University Press, 1965.

Cochrane, Eric, ed. *The Late Italian Renaissance, 1525–1630.* London: Macmillan, 1970.

Cohen, Elizabeth, and Cohen, Thomas V. *Daily Life in Renaissance Italy.* Westport, Conn.: Greenwood Press, 2001.

Cohen, Thomas V. *Love and Death in Renaissance Italy.* Chicago: University of Chicago Press, 2004.

Collins, Amanda. *Greater Than Emperor: Cola di Rienzo (ca. 1313–54) and the World of Fourteenth-Century Rome.* Ann Arbor: University of Michigan Press, 2002.

Creighton, Mandell. *A History of the Papacy from the Great Schism to the Sack of Rome,* 6 vols. London: Longmans, Green, and Co., 1897.

Dandelet, Thomas James. *Spanish Rome, 1500–1700.* New Haven, Conn.: Yale University Press, 2001.

Davis, Charles Till. *Dante and the Idea of Rome.* Oxford, U.K.: Clarendon Press, 1957.

Dickinson, Gladys. *Du Bellay in Rome.* Leiden, Neth.: Brill, 1960.

Gatti, Hilary, ed. *Giordano Bruno: Philosopher of the Renaissance.* Burlington, Vt.: Ashgate, 2002.

Gouwens, Kenneth. *Remembering the Renaissance: Humanist Narratives of the Sack of Rome.* Leiden, Neth.: Brill, 1998.

Gregorovius, Ferdinand. *The Ghetto and the Jews of Rome.* New York: Schocken Books, 1948.

————. *History of the City of Rome in the Middle Ages*, trans. Annie Hamilton, 8 vols. New York: AMS Press, 1967; orig. pub. Stuttgart, 1859–1872.

Harvey, Margaret. *The English in Rome, 1362–1420: Portrait of an Expatriate Community*. Cambridge, U.K.: Cambridge University Press, 1999.

Haskell, Francis. *Patrons and Painters: A Study in the Relations between Italian Art and Society in the Age of the Baroque*, 2nd ed. New Haven, Conn.: Yale University Press, 1980.

Hetherington, Paul. *Medieval Rome: A Portrait of the City and Its Life*. New York: St. Martin's Press, 1994.

Howe, Eunice D. *Andrea Palladio: The Churches of Rome*. Binghamton, N.Y.: Center for Medieval and Early Renaissance Studies, 1991.

Krautheimer, Richard. *Rome: Profile of a City, 312–1308*. Princeton, N.J.: Princeton University Press, 1980.

Lee, Egmont. *Sixtus IV and Men of Letters*. Rome: Edizioni di Storia e Letteratura, 1978.

Maas, Clifford W., and Herde, Peter. *The German Community in Renaissance Rome, 1378–1523*. Rome: Herder, 1981.

Martin, John Jeffries, ed. *The Renaissance: Italy and Abroad*. London and New York: Routledge, 2003.

Masson, Georgina. *Courtesans of the Italian Renaissance*. New York: St. Martin's Press, 1975.

Mazzocco, Angelo, ed. *Interpretations of Renaissance Humanism*. Leiden, Neth.: Brill, 2006.

Mazzoni, Cristina. *She-Wolf: The Story of a Roman Icon*. Cambridge, U.K.: Cambridge University Press, 2010.

Mitchell, Bonner. *Rome in the High Renaissance: The Age of Leo X*. Norman: University of Oklahoma Press, 1973.

Murphy, Caroline. *The Pope's Daughter: The Extraordinary Life of Felice della Rovere*. Oxford, U.K., and New York: Oxford University Press, 2005.

Musto, Ronald G. *Apocalypse in Rome: Cola di Rienzo and the Politics of the New Age*. Berkeley: University of California Press, 2003.

Najemy, John M., ed. *Italy in the Age of the Renaissance: 1300–1550*. Oxford, U.K.: Oxford University Press, 2004.

Nauert, Charles G. *Humanism and the Culture of Renaissance Europe*, 2nd ed. Cambridge, U.K.: Cambridge University Press, 2006.

Nussdorfer, Laurie. *Civic Politics in the Rome of Urban VIII*. Princeton, N.J.: Princeton University Press, 1992.

O'Malley, John W. *Praise and Blame in Renaissance Rome: Rhetoric, Doctrine, and Reform in the Sacred Orators of the Papal Court, c. 1450–1521*. Durham, N.C.: Duke University Press, 1979.

Parks, George Bruner. *The English Traveler to Italy: The Middle Ages (to 1525)*, vol. 1. Rome: Edizioni di Storia e Letteratura, 1954.

————, ed. *Gregory Martin: Roma Sancta (1581)*. Rome: Edizioni di Storia e Letteratura, 1969.

Partner, Peter. *The Lands of St. Peter: The Papal State in the Middle Ages and the Early Renaissance.* Berkeley: University of California Press, 1972.

———. *The Papal State under Martin V: The Administration and Government of the Temporal Power in the Early Fifteenth Century.* London: British School at Rome, 1958.

———. *The Pope's Men: The Papal Civil Service in the Renaissance.* New York: Oxford University Press, 1990.

———. *Renaissance Rome, 1500–1559: A Portrait of a Society.* Berkeley: University of California Press, 1976.

Pastor, Ludwig von. *The History of the Popes, from the Close of the Middle Ages,* trans. F. I. Antrodus, vols. 1–24 for the period through Clement VIII. London: Kegan Paul, Trench, Trübner, & Co., 1899 ff.

Portoghesi, Paolo. *Rome of the Renaissance,* trans. Pearl Sanders. London: Phaidon, 1972.

Ramsey, Paul A. *Rome in the Renaissance: The City and the Myth.* Binghamton, N.Y.: Center for Medieval and Early Renaissance Studies, 1982.

Rowland, Ingrid D., *The Culture of the High Renaissance: Ancients and Moderns in Sixteenth-Century Rome.* Cambridge, U.K.: Cambridge University Press, 1998.

Stinger, Charles L. *The Renaissance in Rome.* Bloomington: Indiana University Press, 1985.

Storey, Tessa. *Carnal Commerce in Counter-Reformation Rome.* Cambridge, U.K., and New York: Cambridge University Press, 2008.

Stow, Kenneth. *Theater of Acculturation: The Roman Ghetto in the Sixteenth Century.* Seattle: University of Washington Press, 2001.

Symonds, John Addington. *A Short History of the Renaissance in Italy,* ed. Alfred Pearson. New York: Cooper Square Publishers, 1966.

Talvacchia, Bette. *Taking Positions: On the Erotic in Renaissance Culture.* Princeton, N.J.: Princeton University Press, 1999.

Young, Norwood. *Rome and its Story,* rev. P. Barrera. London: J. M. Dent & Sons, 1953.

Acknowledgments (*continued from p. iv*)

Figure 1. Photograph courtesy of Cristina Mazzoni.

Figures 2 and 4. Photographs courtesy of Martina Saltamacchia.

Figure 3. Raphael, *Portrait of Pope Julius II*, © National Gallery, London/Art Resource, N.Y.

Document 2. John Wright, tr. Pages 51–53, 134–35, 146–48, and 151–53 from *The Life of Cola di Rienzo*, translated by John Wright (Toronto: The Pontifical Institute of Mediaeval Studies). Copyright © 1975 by the Pontifical Institute of Mediaeval Studies. Reprinted by permission of the Pontifical Institute of Mediaeval Studies.

Document 8. Kenneth Stow. Pages 294–98 from *Catholic Thought and Papal Jewry Policy* by Kenneth Stow (New York: Jewish Theological Seminary). Copyright © 1977 by Jewish Theological Seminary. Reprinted by permission of the Jewish Theological Seminary.

Document 10. Howard Hibbard and Shirley G. Hibbard. Pages 361–62, 364–65, and 367–70 from *Caravaggio* by Howard Hibbard and Shirley G. Hibbard (New York: Westview Press). Copyright © 1985 Howard Hibbard, Shirley G. Hibbard. Reprinted by permission of Westview Press, a member of the Perseus Books Group.

Document 11. Mary D. Garrard, *Artemesia Gentileschi.* © 1989 Princeton University Press. Reprinted by permission of Princeton University Press.

Document 12. William Thomas. Pages 45–53 from *The History of Italy* by William Thomas (Ithaca, N.Y.: Cornell University Press for the Folger Shakespeare Library). Copyright © 1963 by Cornell University Press. Used by permission of the Folger Shakespeare Library.

Document 13. Joachim du Bellay. Pages 137, 171, 175, 179, 181, 213, 219, and 247 from *The Regrets: A Bilingual Edition* by Joachim du Bellay, translated and edited by David R. Slavitt (Evanston, Ill.: Northwestern University Press). Copyright © 2004 by Northwestern University Press. Reprinted by permission of Northwestern University Press.

Document 16. From *The Sack of Rome* by Luigi Guicciardini. Translated and edited by James H. McGregor. New York: Italica Press, 1993. Copyright © 1993 by Italica Press. Used by Permission.

Document 17. Francisco Delicado. Pages 16–18, 37–41, 59–66, 138, and 290–91 from *La Lozana Andaluza* by Francisco Delicado, translated by Bruno M. Damiani (Potomac, Md.: Scripta Humanistica). Copyright © 1987 by Scripta Humanistica. Reprinted by permission of translator Bruno M. Damiani.

Document 19. R. Rosenthal and M. Rosenthal, tr. Pages 231–39 from *Aretino's Dialogues* translated by R. Rosenthal and M. Rosenthal (Toronto: University of Toronto Press). Copyright © 2005 by University of Toronto Press. Reprinted by permission of the publisher.

Document 20. John Longhurst. Pages 20, 22–26, 31, 34–35, 104–5, 109, and 115 from *Alfonso de Valdés and the Sack of Rome* by John Longhurst. Copyright © 1952 University of New Mexico Press.

Document 21. Erasmus. Pages 191–93 in Volume 27, pages 93–94 in Volume 3, pages 197–98 in Volume 5, page 151 in Volume 8, and pages 144–45 in Volume 9 from *Collected Works of Erasmus* (Toronto: University of Toronto Press). Copyright © 1976 by University of Toronto Press. Reprinted by permission of the publisher.

157

Index